KEITH BAIN
The Principles
of Movement

T0321464

Keith Bain teaching at NIDA, 1986 *(Photo: Stuart Campbell, NIDA Archive)*

KEITH BAIN
The Principles
of Movement

Edited by Michael Campbell
Foreword by Cate Blanchett

First published in 2015 by Oberon Books Ltd

521 Caledonian Road, London N7 9RH

Tel: +44 (0) 20 7607 3637 / Fax: +44 (0) 20 7607 3629

e-mail: info@oberonbooks.com

www.oberonbooks.com

A catalogue record for this book is available from the British Library.

PB ISBN: 978-1-78319-109-3

E ISBN: 978-1-78319-608-1

Cover credit: Cate Blanchett in Electra, dir. Lindy Davies, NIDA 1992
(Photo: Marco Bok, NIDA Archive)

also find features, author interviews and news of any author events, and you can sign up for e-newsletters so that you're always first to hear about our new releases.

Contents

Turn your headlights on

A Foreword by
CATE BLANCHETT

I have to admit Keith's was the one class I longed for each week at NIDA. His room was a place of exploration *and* rigorous discipline. When Keith walked in the temperature changed. He would brook no laziness but would support your failure because, in this failure he could sense advancement around the corner: the attempt at what was currently impossible.

I think being a parent I now fully appreciate the generosity and profundity of his pedagogy. His philosophy was to set his students on a path whereby they were equipped and aware enough as actors so that they would no longer need him. His success could only be measured by his invisibility. Most importantly he taught us 'how to learn', so as time passed, jobs came and went, I found myself building, alongside a body of work (and so much more importantly) a technique that allowed me to keep growing as an actor.

The main thing is, when I think about it, he taught me that to be onstage is not merely the learning of lines and characters and accents and limps and crooked hats and fat suits BUT the being available to space and what might happen in that space. How did he do that? It was about energy production and how the impetus to move has to come from somewhere, it must be specific. It was about the power and difference of various aspects of the stage so we could get a sense of what stage pictures could be and the role we played within them. It was about your body in relation to others and of course it was about the audience – what you were actually communicating … all these lessons so key to the theatre, and so important for the immature performer who can get drastically waylaid in turgid personal exploration.

Before encountering Keith I had a free-floating love and interest in dance (I had this dream of joining Pina Bausch in Wupperthal) and a very separate—but equally pressing—interest in drama and the creation of character. He synthesised these two urges in me (and in many students at NIDA) and he facilitated the genuine exploration where these two passions and approaches to performance could intermingle and cross-fertilise. Drama school can be a nightmarish labyrinth where you have a separate and confusing experience in each class, whereas his training enabled all the different strands, passions, yearnings and influences to interconnect and inter-relate.

When teaching a class, Keith himself was mischievous, up for it, twinkling of eye, ready for change and challenge. A boon and a blessing, a peer and a pedagogue, a shining beacon whose approval we all desperately sought. In this book there is the opportunity to grapple with his process in great detail. It takes you clearly through his approaches, methodology—more concerned with why to do an exercise than how to do an exercise. The power and import of this book lies in its benefit to practitioners, teachers, oddbods interested in the practice of theatre and 'odderbods' concerned with the history of performance in Australia on which Keith has undoubtedly had a lasting impact. Speaking personally there is no doubt Keith was and is the biggest single influence on my work as an actor; and my guess is on all of us who were taught by him. This book is for those poor buggers who didn't get it on the floor.

Introduction

MICHAEL CAMPBELL

Keith Bain (1926-2012) was one of Australia's most influential theatre practitioners and a mentor to generations. Over the course of a lifetime as an actor, dancer, teacher, movement director and choreographer, he developed a comprehensive and unique approach to the complexities of human movement within the theatrical context.

His teachings have been literally embodied by numerous generations of performers, and have guided and inspired many of Australia's most notable actors and directors, among them Geoffrey Rush, Mel Gibson, Judy Davis, Miranda Otto, Richard Roxburgh, Jim Sharman and Gale Edwards. The success of Keith's approach is evident both in their work and in the recollections included in this book.

The reason his approach to Movement is so successful in its practical application is that he never declared a 'Bain technique'. He doesn't offer a codified system of instructions and exercises. His approach presents a rigorous, highly practical, theoretical framework and a structured series of questions and investigations that builds personal awareness and provides the performer with the necessary tools to master their body as the fundamental instrument of their expression on stage, on camera and in life.

Keith believed the best way to learn is experientially. The source material for his investigations into movement is eclectic and inclusive, drawing upon the many techniques and body sciences, such as mime, martial arts, ballet, ballroom dancing, gymnastics, circus skills, yoga,

Laban, Feldenkrais, Alexander, Suzuki, kinesiology, biomechanics. Each lesson is an opportunity to discover and experiment; a step towards building a strong sense of the body's capabilities and potential, as well as a robust set of personal beliefs. A teacher of Keith's approach uses the prism of their own movement training and experience to build the student's own awareness and capability. Students of 'Keith' learn how to learn for themselves.

The Bain approach is 'bigger' and more far-reaching than any single methodology. This is one of its core strengths. The only reason his teachings are less widely known than those of Laban and Feldenkrais, is that they have remained unpublished – until now.

Acknowledgements

Everyone has their own personal Keith. He revealed to us our potential as teachers, performers and people. But more than that, without 'teaching' us, he instilled the tools within us so that we could realise the profound nature of our transformations. He taught us not to need him; but the truth is, all those who entered his classroom or rehearsal studio carry him within us – in the way we move and in our fascination with the intersection of life and art.

When Keith was formulating the National Institute of Dramatic Art's post-graduate Movement Studies course in 1990 he began thinking about writing a book that contained his approach, philosophy and beliefs about Movement. For a man who was so eloquent and economical with words when teaching or rehearsing he found the act of writing immensely difficult. Eventually he put work on the book aside. Some years later a group of former students and colleagues approached me to become involved in seeing this work come to fruition. Having completed the Movement Studies course in 1994 and subsequently also become involved in the world of books and literature, it seemed a natural choice. The manuscript needed restructuring and many sections were left unfinished. In order to complete the work I drew upon Keith's class notes, articles, interviews, several oral histories, Anca Frankenhauser who chose Keith as the subject for her Masters of Dramatic Art (Movement Studies) thesis, and the recollections of one of Keith's closest colleagues, Julia Cotton.

In 2010 Currency House published *Keith Bain on Movement*. This book also covered material most relevant to teachers, choreographers, movement directors, directors and other performing arts practitioners. It became a tribute for all the students that knew him as one of their most treasured teachers, but little of the man himself. The inclusion of his biography contextualised the wisdom he imparted.

For *The Principles of Movement* a different approach was needed; one that would talk to students in the most practical way to assist them in mastering the potential and remarkable capabilities Keith's Movement can offer. I restructured and edited the original content to focus it more acutely on the needs of the student of acting. There are more framed exercises to assist the student to translate Keith's theory into practice and I have changed 'the voice', so Keith talks directly to the reader, making the experience of the book more intimate.

There are many acknowledgements:

The Australia Council for awarding Keith an Australian Creative Artist's Creative Fellowship to begin the initial work on the book. The Keith Bain Book Team whose joint experience, energy and commitment allowed the first edition of the book to be realised: Elizabeth Butcher, Donato Carretti, Dean Carey, Julia Cotton, Nicholas Flanagan, Anca Frankenhauser, Lee James, Sheree James, Odile Le Clezio, Raymond Mather, Arky Michael, Dean Nottle, Wendy Parson, Jill Sykes, Christine Roberts.

To those who assisted in the research and the sourcing of the photographs: Dr Margaret Leask (providing oral history tapes), Dr Peter Orlovich (Seaborn, Broughton and Walford Foundation Archives), Vicki Brown, Malcolm Forbes, Ann O'Hea and Beris Tomkins (NIDA archives), Judith Seeff (Sydney Theatre Company archives), Harry M. Miller, Richard Stone and the Robert Walker Estate.

To all the donors that made *Keith Bain on Movement* possible, in particular Ros Horin and Joe Skrzynski who enabled many of the other donations. Also Keith's long-time dance partner, Joyce Lofts who actively fundraised. Thank you too to all those who contributed the quotations included in this book; the National Institute of Dramatic Art at which

Keith worked for over thirty-five years; and all those who have cared for Keith as his health became less robust.

To all those at Currency House, and in particular Katharine Brisbane, Priscilla Yates, Claire Grady and Emma Vine, as well as Melina Theocharidou at Oberon Books.

We all hope that within the pages of this new edition people will find inspiration, understanding and tools with which to approach the art and craft of performing, and life.

PART I
The Principles

1

What is Movement?

Keith established Movement as a unique discipline central to actor training. His influence on Australian theatre will continue for many years to come.

JOHN CLARK AND ELIZABETH BUTCHER

What's the big deal?

We all move, so what is the big deal? We move when we want to. Get where we need to go without thinking much about it. We have little regard for how awkwardly or gracelessly we do it. So why get into a state about it?

We are constantly speaking a movement language—the language of our own individual life—that is transparently readable. In ordinary life, we picked up this language in so informal a fashion that although we can make ourselves reasonably understood, we speak it with the limited effectiveness of a person who is using a language but is ignorant of its spelling and grammar.

Movement is both how we move and what moves us. Movement is the look in our eyes, the tensions and the tone in our muscles, our breathing, our thinking, our longings and fears. Movement Studies has equal concern for the inner and the outer aspects, with each clarifying the other, enriching the connections and, like all knowledge, extending the imaginative and artistic horizons. There are psychological implications underlying all the movements we make and all of the theories, concepts and analytical principles that are currently in practice: and there are possibilities and manifestations of movement to be investigated in the actor's search for the revelation of psychological truth and inner richness.

What is Movement?

Movement is a big subject and demands a big definition. But precisely because its range is so wide, it is difficult to give it a simple definition. Movement is capable of the finest shades of everything, from delicacy and ecstasy to grossness and abstraction. Its implications are so essential to everything we do that it is vital to the whole organic art and craft of performance.

'Movement for actors' can be a vague and threatening term to people who don't consider themselves physically adept or experienced. Many find exercise boring and may have spent a lifetime avoiding it. Others may be prejudiced against physical activity of any kind, as a result of accident or humiliation in the playground or on the sports field. These are the ones who imagine the study of Movement will expose an even more depressing array of physical and expressive deficiencies than those of which they are too well aware. For others again, the idea of Movement will have been coloured by a damaged self-image composed of a nasty combination of former criticisms, failures, poor or insensitive teaching, cruel taunts and a dislike of their own body, looks and general physicality.

The popular perception is that Movement training is mostly a matter of teaching actors to faint and fall down stairs, dance a little, bow and curtsy elegantly, be capable of some mime and stage fighting. People think that the word dance is a helpful one, and they think dance and Movement are essentially the same thing. Unfortunately that is not the case. When an actor acts well, the physicalisation of the actor's inner and outer life is so seamless, truthful and discreet that it all looks as though movement just happens. A virtuoso technique can disguise the effort. When an actor acts less well, when the body tells lies and fails to find ease and truth, the significance of Movement becomes clear.

Sadly, relatively few people, even actors themselves, fully appreciate the potential of the study of Movement. Top directors, and company administrators for drama, opera and film, see value in dramaturgs and voice consultants but fail to involve a Movement specialist in a production except to deal with the dance sequence or the sword fight. In doing so, they fail to appreciate the enormous contribution an expert in Movement can bring to a production, enriching the actors' choices, setting the style of the piece and its concept, refining the atmospheres and creating the dramatic visualisation of the whole production.

We moved before we painted, carved, danced or sang. And yet, probably because our movement is so basic to us and so bound up with ordinariness and practicality, we have taken a long time to see the art in it and the beauty that comes from its truthfulness. The component building blocks of all the principal art forms have been set for centuries. These elements have provided a basis for criticism, comparison and, importantly, become the groundwork for practical approaches to the teaching of that art form.

Music in Western civilisations, for example, has long been defined as consisting of melody, harmony, rhythm, form, instrumental colour and dynamics. These are perfect bases for study, for evaluation, for developing teaching techniques for composition and performance and for creating the notation system that preserves the music of every period. For thousands of years, in hundreds of cultures, sculpture has been defined as space, perspective, proportion, texture and composition. Around the art form a theory and a set of practices and principles have developed that heighten the appreciation of it, and build traditions that can be taught to each new generation of sculptors. In painting, the elements of colour, design, perspective, tone and form have been explored to the advantage of artists, scholars, historians, critics, teachers and their students.

Think now of such essentials to the study of Movement as motive, instinct, intention, inspiration, time, energy, emotion and temperament, and it becomes clear how intangible these are until they are examined by the results they produce.

François Delsarte, (1811–1871)* made a brave attempt at a philosophy of Movement. He claimed that movement could be classified into three distinct categories: mental (the head), emotional (the trunk) and physical (the limbs); and his three laws: of opposition, natural succession and harmonic positions, created considerable interest among his contemporaries. He sought to make a complete analysis of the gestures and movements of the human body and attempted to formulate laws of speech and gesture that would be as precise as mathematical principles. For him, the artist's aim should be to move, interest and persuade; and he considered that nothing could be more deplorable than a gesture without motive.† Though his work is of little influence today, he provoked fresh thought, especially among the early wave of Central European modern dancers, including Mary Wigman, Kurt Jooss and Laban himself.

The genius who saw through all the blurring layers was Rudolf Laban (1879–1958). His discoveries changed everything. He has influenced dance and choreography, drama production and drama training, therapy through movement, the notating of dance and movement works, the analysis of Movement qualities in the human and natural spheres and much more. That his conclusions burst onto the European arts scene so long after all the other art forms had been formulated, accounts for the ongoing struggle for academic acceptance that dance and theatre educationalists continue to face.

---

*   See Ted Shawn, *Every Little Movement, A Book About Delsarte*. Princeton, NJ: Princeton Book Co. 1976; and John w. Zorn, *The Essential Delsarte*, Metuchen, N J: Scarecrow Press 1968.

†   See Marie Cuckson, *The New Dance: Gertrude Bodenwieser*. Sydney: Marie Cuckson private edition, 1964, as well as from Bodenwieser herself.

Gertrud Bodenwieser (1890–1959) was one of those pioneers who readily acknowledged his contribution to her own thinking, as she acknowledged the work of another historic figure in the history of movement theorists, Emile Jacques–Dalcroze (1865–1959). Dalcroze set out to investigate new ways of teaching music, and particularly rhythm, which he claimed to be the basis of art. His system involved translating sound into movement, and in doing so he introduced the concepts of space and speed, timing, levels and force, to the world of movement and dance. He also believed that the study of gymnastics, musical theory and rhythm was fundamentally important for physical and moral balance.

The two categories of Movement

Movement ranges from absolute stillness, through the simplest of natural movements to feats of skill that lie beyond the capacity of any but the rarest of individuals. However, there is a clear twofold division. Helen Cameron and Diana Kendall in their book *Kinetic Sensory Studies* distinguish the first category as Survival Movement.* The second can be defined as Learned Skills and Practices.

Survival Movement

Survival Movement has to do with the basics, and refinements, of all the natural and practical movement that evolution has deemed necessary. It includes obvious things like mastering the features and dimensions of our own structure. It encompasses not only all the most basic activities—walking, running, grasping, climbing, pulling, pushing and so on—but also communicating with others, satisfying our needs and pleasures, and adapting to the varying conditions of existence, such as hunting, gathering and building. It is a treasure trove.

---

* Helen Cameron and Diana Kendall, *Kinetic Sensory Studies: A movement program for Children.* Canberra: Published by the authors, 1986

The word 'movement' immediately indicates its concern with doing. Doing anything—from the subtlest involvement of the small muscle groups to the most violent and extravagant response to a situation. Doing nothing is a positive aspect of moving. Whatever you are doing right now, whatever you have just been doing, and whatever you do next, either planned or unforeseen, is the stuff of Movement. Whether your movement develops from within your mood, need or will, or is a reaction to an external stimulus, it is all part of the study.

Even the most ordinary activities, such as how you sit, stand, walk, gesture, eat, drink, scratch, fix your hair, turn the page, frown, smile, chew your fingernail, carry your head, wear your clothes, are movements telling the moment by moment story of your nature and your life as you live it. The angles of your body, your distance from your partner, how often you blink, are all revealing details. More significant, in Movement terms, is how these activities change and adjust to each new inner impulse and each outer change of circumstance. A big implication here for the actor is how you might adjust, modify, and refine movement to better effect.

Learned skills and practices

The second category includes whatever skills and practices humans, over time and within their special circumstances, have invented and developed. Man's ingenuity and capacity for play and expression have seen to it that there are a myriad of these devised skills and practices. They include all dance forms, circus skills, the many types of sports, yoga and the various martial arts. These skills require focus, coordination, timing, strength and agility, often stamina and endurance. They are consciously performed actions that require repetition and practice to become proficient and can reach unbelievably high standards of complexity, artificiality and sophistication.

For ease, I define everything concerning survival movement as Movement with a capital M, and therefore the subject of Movement Studies. All the devised forms are just other ways to move.

Keith, studio shot 1974

Applications of Movement

Reconstructing, in a performing situation, the inner and outer truth of even the least complicated sequence of natural activity, is fiendishly difficult. If, as an actor, all you ever performed was a character exactly like yourself, it would still be difficult to present that character with naturalness and honesty in front of an audience or camera. It would mean being free of all your inhibitions and secure in awareness of your personal reactions, mannerisms, and the physical manifestations of your emotional and psychological states. To reproduce it in all its honesty we need the capacity to analyse what we do. As an actor, however, you are habitually faced with representing a variety of characters. So you need to be as wise and sensitive about others, as you are about yourself. The study of Movement allows an acting technique that is grounded in the analysis of your own behaviour patterns, psychological states and the dictates of your temperament, yet allows the ability to experiment with the underlying principles of acting.

As a physical and practical study, Movement should include, but not be confined to, the mechanical and the technical considerations of a body in motion. Its ultimate forms are disciplined expressiveness, transformational ability and insightful human behaviour. Look those up in your dictionary and the subject of Movement, in all its glory and responsibility, will be revealed.

Movement as evidence of the internal world

Concern for the naturalistic detail of behavioural patterns, and the reproduction of realism in stage movement, however, has its counterbalance. 'Truth' is not necessarily best expressed by naturalistic means. The stage, often more so than film and television, can make its strongest and most telling statements by departure from the natural and the literal into degrees of stylisation, enlargement, distortion, symbolism and abstraction that can enrich immeasurably the presentation of character and narrative, and the depiction of powerful atmospheres. The simply personal can be made universal when these devices are employed, but only when actors are capable of heightening the truth of their inner states in the playing of them. This must not mean that the actor is leaving truth further and further behind as they move deeper into an abstracted or stylised state. It should be that they are entering deeper into the essence of that truth, intensifying it as they go. This presents many an actor with a considerable challenge. For instance, young actors who can comfortably represent the truth of contemporary characters and situations, find the truth of an unfamiliar time and place, with its own perspectives, protocol, etiquette and conventions, an inhibition to making artistic judgment. It requires the actor to be both brave and at ease when they are given the challenge of exploring extremes of eccentricity, grandeur, stillness, vulnerability and abstracted states.

We cannot see a thought but movement can give evidence, not only of the process of thinking but of the nature of that thought. We cannot directly see an emotion, or such physical states as pain and hunger, or such characteristics as greed or shyness, but we can recognise, through the evidence of movement, precise and precious detail of all these experiences as well as the changing degrees of their intensity. It is movement, perhaps as discreet as a pause in one's breathing or an introverted focus of the eye, that reveals all these states.

Three points to consider in this regard are of great importance:

- The constant change of thought and feeling as we succeed or fail to achieve what we want;
- The very moments of change from one degree of feeling to another, and from one state of thinking to another;
- The degree to which we either reveal or conceal our motives and their accompanying emotional states.

All of these considerations involve some of the subtlest aspects of movement for the actor. The capacity to manifest these in performance is the mark of our finest actors.

By the first of these points, I refer to the need for the actor to realise that though their state of feeling or thinking—for example anger over a failure to get what they want from another person—may last for several minutes, it changes every few seconds in its degree. Actors often tend to see their scenes in generalised terms, for example the sad scene, the angry scene. They maintain their sadness at a consistent level for as long as that section lasts. But, in response to all that is happening and is being said, that anger will flare and blaze at one moment, subside at another, slowly build and reach a climax of fury, or perhaps reduce in intensity to a lesser but controllable agitation. It may rage out of control at times and be partly suppressed a minute later. But neither anger nor sadness, nor any emotion, is a fixed or measured commodity. A line-graph of anger would range from the first release of heat through the body to an unstoppable rage that leads to violence. It is not truthful or dramatically interesting for an actor to register a fixed reading on their emotional pressure gauge, and no audience wants to be subjected to a long scene delivered on one protracted emotional note.

The second point deals with the moment of change. This is that vulnerable, dramatically rich moment when one state of feeling, thinking, sensing, of dynamics or atmosphere, is replaced by another. Regardless of whether this raises or lowers the energy level of the scene, it is a contrast, a new colour to be savoured, a fresh detail or perspective that keeps the scene alive and provides a strong sense of spontaneity. It is that instant when an answer to the problem flashes into the mind; when what has been clear and acceptable is suddenly seen as complex and suspicious; when a word or a look or an action breaks one atmosphere and a new one invades the scene. It is present when, in the text, another issue is introduced, or when a character tries another ploy to get what they want. Many actors fail to register the number and the variety of such moments of change. They ride over the top of precious opportunities that can chart for an audience the pattern of inner activity taking place within the character. And since these inner changes create outer and visible reactions, the actor robs himself of movement details that carry within them a richer and more precise truth.

The third point concerns the degree to which we reveal or conceal our motives and their accompanying emotional states. The effort involved in the concealment or revelation of the inner life will be evident through our body and its actions. I prefer actors whose work is never generalised, whose inner and outer details of characterisation succeed in revealing how many insightful ways people differ from one another. In the first moments of such an actor's appearance on the stage, long before a word is spoken, the audience has absorbed information by the tonne.

Whether they remain in the doorway or stride into the centre; the age, shape, size, colouring of that actor—even the angle of the body, their posture and position within the stage space, the facial expression, the light in their eye, how they wear their clothes—are details that are quickly absorbed by an audience. The visible details will be translated by the viewer to represent the inner qualities and attributes which created those externals in the first place. When that actor moves—at whatever speed, in whatever direction and with whatever dynamic or gesture—the story grows, the atmosphere changes and the mood and motive is revealed. Appetites and energies, self-image, temperament, likes and dislikes can be revealed in dramatic movement with more accuracy, speed and truthfulness than through pages of dialogue. When both movement and text are respected, and when they come together, we get close to heaven.

All of this could be described in a single word, 'behaviour'. It is in our behaviour that all our inner and outer qualities meet. It is where our particular brew of moods, drives, attitudes and appetites connect with our physicality and intellect to produce action. It is our response in our active life, to our heredity and our conditioning. It is on the basis of our behaviour that other people read us: like us, loathe us, want us, ignore us, manipulate us, trust or suspect us, treasure or undervalue us. Researching the character through the text should lead you to a presentation of behaviour that tells the audience all it needs to know. It helps to be a student of life—not just borrowing behavioural patterns but going deeper to find the essence of what people reveal by the way they behave.

How differently each of us reacts to a single set of conditions; how inconsistently we behave even when the circumstances are similar. How differently our moods, and the obstacles we face, change the way we conduct ourselves, how we treat others and respond to the way that others treat us. Behaviour is about how we go about getting what we want. It is how we choose to deal with what life throws at us. It is the best evidence of who we are.

The language of Movement

The first meeting with someone new leaves us with a detailed impression that will colour our feelings about that person, maybe for life. The knowledge that our every appearance carries such significant data should alert us to a range of challenging implications. Movement Studies can explore how characters differ from each other in their expression of energy, which is a manifestation of an inner life on the following levels: physical, intellectual, sensory, sexual, nervous, emotional, spiritual, imaginative and creative.

There is a Movement language that allows an actor to disclose those aspects of a character's status and temperament that become apparent from the study of the script. The performer needs to become expert at extracting from the text insightful information about all these details. Movement details and choices allow the actors to pinpoint the period,

Bitter Sweet: Dir. Robin Lovejoy, Movement Keith Bain, NIDA 1982.

the social class and the status of the role they are playing. Through subtle adjustments to their physicality, body angles, spatial relationships, body language and facial expressions, actors can make these distinctions clear to an audience. Moreover, a good actor's body can establish the degrees of intimacy and varying relationships that exist among the playwright's cast of characters.

Dance and Movement

Dance technique does not necessarily make actors better actors. Quite often dance is taught in a way that overvalues form, externals, style and presentation. Its approaches to characterisation often lead to superficial and stereotypic results based on generalised analysis of the circumstances, relationships and motivation. It can produce mannerisms, ideal perhaps for some dance styles, but undesirable for an actor seeking a neutral, adjustable physicality. The need to conform to the strict style and physicality of each dance form can rob a student of his or her precious individual qualities. It can become difficult for dance students to find their own vocabulary and language of movement outside the vocabulary of dance. So much so that the extent of their physical courage, spontaneity and creativity is diminished. The defined positions, gestures and body shapes of dance can become movements to hide behind, to feel safe in, rather than the means of organically expressing and bravely transmitting and receiving the aspects of inner life that are the actor's task and joy.

Dance is mostly a matter of right and wrong in the essential areas of timing and rhythm, spatial definition,

I had done some dance before. I thought I would have a bit of an advantage in the Movement area. And yet I didn't. Somehow my dancing didn't really help me at the Movement class at all. Occasionally if we had to do a bit of dancing it came in handy that I could learn choreography. But Movement is something else entirely. It's just being able to watch the way people move. Movement is going on all the time. Dance is a very selective, little, part of Movement.

MIRANDA OTTO

*I really became aware of Keith when
we did a summer seminar in Armidale.
I remember being so amazed because
he did this solo improvisation and
at one stage he just moved his little
finger, and it was the most telling
movement, and the biggest movement
I'd ever seen. I was very impressed.*

GARTH WELCH

*Keith showed me how to make a human
being move, because we expect a
dancer to have a neutral body and to
fit into a mould. Keith showed me that
there is something amazingly special
about every individual body. And it is
the way that each body finds movement
which is really special. And in a way
that, had you planned it, you would
never have found that amount of detail.*

JANE MISKOVIC

*He has an empathetic response to
actors and acting. It was his phrase,
'scared eyes' that alerted us to the
actor who, rather than taking charge of
the audience, was letting the audience
take charge. He is a demanding critic,
and generous when generosity is
deserved. I found that we ignored his
criticisms and suggestions at our peril.*

TERENCE CLARKE

shape, alignment, dynamics and body
details. It can easily ignore the exploration of even greater dynamic range, of
dramatic rather than metrical rhythms,
of personal style, of emotional courage
and access to emotion, as well as the
processes of transformation, personalisation and psychological revelation.

Physical skills

Important, but to me less so, are the
dozens of extra skills, such as dance,
fencing, and gymnastics, that add
dimension and range to the actor but
which I believe are supplementary to the
core of an actor's Movement. This does

Drew Forsythe in *The Venetian Twins*. Dir. John
Bell, Music Terence Clarke, Chor. Keith Bain,
Sydney Theatre Company 1979.

not deny their value when used in modified forms to develop special qualities and degrees of self-awareness and discovery. I would love to have the knowhow and the time to make my students proficient in abseiling, horse riding, Swedish massage, stunt work, Graham technique, skiing, fencing, uni-cycling, ballroom dancing and meditation, Indian dance and bungy-jumping. But none of these reach into the heart of the actor's work.

There used to be many drama schools that gave Movement courses based almost exclusively on any one of these recognised techniques. All the schools in which I have taught would have been happy enough for me to do just that. No performer can have too many areas of expertise. Skills are essential, but they are only part of the Movement story.

2

A System of Beliefs

In the field of teaching Keith Bain is one of the most inspiring and influential Australian Masters. Keith's work encompasses many aspects of contemporary acting techniques, sometimes superseding them.

TONY KNIGHT

In my view there is no such thing as a 'Bain technique', unless my eclecticism in itself is a technique. I have picked up ideas from sources I can hardly trace now and added them to discoveries of my own, all the time replacing approaches that didn't quite work and testing out new ones. Slowly I refined my process, adding and eliminating in the light of new knowledge, experiment and discovery. The changes in the classes I offered to each new generation of students have been so radical that anyone I taught even six or seven years ago would see great differences, not only in the priorities and inclusions of my present class structure but also my use of words and images. What they might still recognise would be my beliefs. In fact my system is defined by my beliefs; and beliefs need to be constantly validated and updated to be the driving force that makes them such a strong element of teaching.

My starting point is the human condition: the wonder and potential of the body; our motivations and behaviours; the miracle of our
complexity; the comedy and tragedy of faults and feelings; the tangle
of our emotional and psychological inner life; the contradictions of
potential and realisation; and the life forces that propel us. The logic
of theatre arts is not so different from life, in that common sense,
open-mindedness, worldly wisdom and a sense of proportion can only
help in solving artistic problems.

The following set of beliefs is a very personal list, and for many
who read this it may prove most useful as a tool for argument and
challenge. Never think of the examples I give as being anything but
examples. There are no fixed rules. I believe strongly in a scientific base
for the work but I recognise that I am no scientist and have added no
scientific advancements to the study. I am curious about, and grateful
for, the theories and the theorists that have revealed the underlying
principles of human movement. Yet no single theory has become the
basis for my approach. In fact, I prefer to teach in a way that exposes,
rather than illustrates, a theoretical foundation.

I am uncomfortable with the metaphysical, the esoteric, the transcendental. I seldom, if ever, use abstract images, words or concepts
like 'soul', 'spirit', or 'psyche'. This is because I am never certain that
the meaning I give to these words is, in any way, similar to that which
others give. But I think it is essential to have a set of beliefs at the
core of our technique, and it is those beliefs that will lead each of us,
through experimentation, to formulate the system that will suit us best.

The eloquence of the body

The body is always saying something. It cannot say nothing. Even a dead
body tells us it is dead. Each performer, from inside their own body,
needs to know that their body can be read for the truthfulness of each
moment. An audience can tell when an actor's focus lacks attention,
when the emotional state presented is a lie; whether the actor is in or

out of the moment, is securely centred or ill at ease, or when the body fails to give evidence of the actor's full and ever-changing inner life. Simply stated, since the body, its shape, use of space, time and dynamics, is always making a statement, it had better be making the appropriate one. Appropriate and inappropriate are the operative words here, rather than right or wrong. Every statement by the body-mind will have its appropriate moment and its most appropriate body manifestation. 'Wrong', as an evaluation of a physical response to a point in performance, suggests that acting is a matter of 'right' choices and reactions.

Certain styles of production do, of course, demand technical correctness. In music theatre you are either on the beat, and the note, or not. In dance the foot is either pointed or it is not. In physical theatre there had better be no wrong judgments of space and timing when launching into a leap or when catching a partner. In any formal stage presentation, a line of bodies is straight or it is not; a circle is a circle or it is not. But when it comes to expressing the specifics of an inner life, such hard and fast rules don't apply. Happy, angry, sad, proud are all generalisations that on their own mean nothing to an actor.

Great painters understand the statements of which a body is capable. Their powers of observation allow them to analyse and then reproduce the infinite subtleties of expression of their subjects. These can be read by the viewer—often more tellingly from dead paint on a dead canvas than from a living person. Sculptors can be dramatists too, coaxing warm life and recognizable feelings from their cold material. Standing in St Peter's in Rome in front of the Michelangelo *Pieta* I marvelled at the artistry that drew out of a block of marble the heavy death of the Son and the life, love and loss of the Mother, as well as at the artist's choreographic eye and director's discernment as he extracts the truth of that moment from the total form of the piece and its multitude of tiny details. I also envy the accuracy and perception of cartoonists who, with a couple of swift strokes, can pinpoint personality traits and express a miraculous range of emotions. Their skill in accentuating and manipulating the visible aspects of movement possibilities to expose the inner working of their characters' lives, derives largely from their gift of

Keith with dance partner Joyce Lofts.

What we tried to do was dance in a truly genuine way. It was controversial because we were the first dancers to come out of American training and work and compete under the English system. They didn't like it! But the public loved us.

JOYCE LOFTS

recognising the exact spot in the body that carries the focus for each moment and reaction. They can spot the angle of the head that denotes the snob or the lover, the drawn-down corners of a cruel mouth, the splayed legs and reinforced chest of the aggressor and the dizziness of Cupid's latest victim. Much of this detail is stereotype, and the main technique is distortion, but the best of the world's cartoonists and animators are uncannily accurate in their observations of us in action. They seem to perceive these elements more precisely than actors or dancers experience them.

Acting is Movement

Thinking, feeling, sensing, knowing, not knowing, is movement. Speaking is movement. So is stillness. These, and many other states and degrees of feeling, are often expressed by movement of such smallness, subtlety and precise placement in the body that it requires of an actor great sensitivity and refinement.

Emotional centres and release points

Emotional centres are those body regions that are the home base for our feelings and control the varying intensity of these feelings. Release points are those places through which we transmit our inner statements and communicate them to other people. I experience my pleasurable and my hateful responses as living in quite different centres in my torso. My likings expand the space in my chest; dread and guilt contract that space and reshape my entire upper body. Surprises, pleasant or unpleasant, suspend my breath and produce a backward and upward impulse. Grief and despair can hit me in the belly, in the guts, while a deeper centre in the pit of the stomach seems to register feelings

Keith wasn't only adept at interpreting and transforming the physical, he had the ability to season and ignite all the senses. This significantly enhanced the potential of the physical.
SUSAN BARLING

of disgust and repugnance. Increases and diminutions in the intensity of any feeling may produce big shifts in reaction from one emotional centre to another.

If you are having trouble with what I am describing, try a thought process like this. What if you entered a familiar space without anticipating any discovery, pleasant or otherwise? Be surprised and then curious at finding someone you don't recognise lying dead on the floor. Imagine then the shock of recognising them to be someone you know but don't like, and then the greater shock of identifying them as someone you know and like very much. Let your inner monologue take you from hope that there is nothing serious to be dealt with, through panic and indecision about the best course of action, to the horror of realising that you are faced with a tragedy that is worse than you ever imagined. It is a corny story but the progression of states of feeling will allow you to trace a sequence of body centres activated in turn.

Poets and novelists for centuries have described the emotional states of their heroes, villains and lovers in terms of their beating hearts, held breaths, collapsing chests, parting lips, staring eyes. These are effective literary conceits because they are universally recognisable and produce in the reader an empathetic response when the writer succeeds in pinpointing an emotional centre.

The head, including the face and the voice, is certainly one such centre. For many actors it is the most overworked. So often I have watched heads, faces and eyes made to do all the work while the rest of the body hardly registers the emotions demanded by the script. Working with emotion while wearing a neutral mask can reveal how unresponsive bodies can be and how much of our body language is reduced when the

John Bell and Keith Bain at rehearsals for *Candide,* Nimrod Theatre Company 1981.

face is no longer allowed to be the focus of our expressive equipment. The face is so mobile and busy that we so often use it as if it represents the whole of us. No wonder we are so much more aware of it than we are of the rest of our body.

The body as a transmitter and receiver

The act of acting is very much the expression of ideas, desires, intentions and states of feeling, energies and appetites, all of which must be released to clear points of focus, through clearly defined distances, for the perfect acceptance and understanding of an eager audience. The skill of projecting these messages has also to be balanced with the capacity to receive, invite, absorb, take in and feed on, information from without. Other aspects of this process include the body's capacity to reject, ignore, block, deny. I keep finding more and more release points through which the transmission of outgoing messages can take place, and open windows and catchment areas through which incoming information can be gathered. There is hardly a part of us, or an angle, that can't be used as a barrier, a threat, a wall against unwelcome attention. And yet these same body areas that send the message of warning and denial can suddenly function as the magnet and become the very spot that receives what is being offered.

To be able to have feedback that makes a difference to you can only happen when someone is sending the signal out and is able to receive the signal back. Keith carries that with him wherever he goes, wherever he teaches. I have seen a room light up because suddenly the possibility of possibility itself is present.

DEAN CAREY

The dynamic centre

Within each of us is a particular spot from which we produce the energy force that propels us into action. Watching people in a simple activity like walking, especially observing them break stillness to take the first step, makes clear how many variations there are in the location of their individual dynamic centre.

The range extends from the person whose head leads off, almost towing his body along, to the leg walker whose torso sits like a passenger on a pair of legs. In one the head is clearly making all the choices and dictating the energy levels and the posture line to the rest of the body, in the other it's the legs that seem to have made all the decisions and have not bothered to let the rest of the body know. In between are the shoulder people whose one or both shoulders launch them into action, often with a lurch or a roll; chest people, whose real, or inflated, sense of self can be read in their manner of driving out from a chest pumped up by a projecting power. Others are powered variously by heightened animation and high energy level at the hips, in the pelvic and genital region, the buttocks, the belly, the spine, even the arms, the elbows, the wrists, the hand, the forehead, the eye and the jaw.

Take each of these examples for a walk by imagining your dynamic centre in each of these places. Observe how it feels, and how it changes your outlook on the world.

Self-knowledge

Intelligence and knowledge are indispensable assets but what is understood by the head, must be revealed through the body. Actors whom we recognise as ineffectual are not necessarily lacking in insight or intellect. Quite often I have found them to have a clear grasp of acting theory and to be the most painstaking members of the class or cast. They may understand every detail of the play's theme and structure, as well as the character's function and journey through the piece, and have researched the dramatic possibilities till they are as informed about all aspects of the piece as the director and the dramaturg put together. The root of their problem is limited self-perception.

Since an actor needs only to play the differences between himself and the character that he portrays, his problem could well be not knowing himself with sufficient intimacy, in terms of physicality, dynamic range, temperament and personal mannerisms, for those differences to be clear and revealed through action. And it is not enough for this knowledge to be primarily behavioural. Just as crucial is his sense of identity, realised in the myriad facets of daily role-playing—and in the admirable and shameful qualities behind our thinking and our actions.

Two main ways to approach a new characterisation continue to be debated: from the outside in or from the inside out. Many great actors prefer one approach over the other. Surely the ideal way is the one that works best for you. Besides, neither way of working succeeds if it does not connect to the other. Unless the outer manifestations, that might include body displacements and re-shapings, selected gestures, articles of clothing and personal effects, have the effect of changing the actor's inner life and perceptions, then the characterisation will remain external and cosmetic. Similarly, unless the interior, psychological preparation achieves an outer manifestation that allows that inner world to be released, it will appear that there is no inner story to be told. It makes sense to me for an actor to employ any and every means available to build and enrich their characters. In one role externals may awaken the richest response. In another the opposite could achieve the most. Perhaps a combination is the greatest solution. I have vivid memories of Robyn Nevin, one of our finest actresses, and how she would feel unable to release the complex inner realities of her characters until she had found the right shoes and the right hair-do. Then everything connected and the transformation took place.

As a teacher I allow experiments that give students a choice in their methodology.

EXERCISE IN EXPERIENCING MOTIVATION

Start on one side of the space and find a point of focus on the opposite side. Then simply walk directly towards it; when you arrive pause, turn around and find another point of focus across the room and walk towards it. Continue in this way, criss-crossing the space with different journeys. Experiment by taking different speeds for each journey, slowing down or speeding up, pausing somewhere along the way. Try indirect pathways as well as direct. Make the point of focus on the ground or higher up to explore different levels. With each change allow yourself to be affected: imagine different circumstances for each journey. You can experiment with combining any of these elements and discover a different story each time you traverse the space. Also consider the difference between departing and arriving. You can endow your point of focus with a place or person. You can also explore moving away from, as well as towards, your point of focus.

From a very simple exercise you will find that just small alterations affect the motivation and (with imagination) it generally works well.

JULIA COTTON

Empathetic observation

As an actor, being a curious and informed student of life in general, and mankind in particular, is the starting point to the refined skill of observational analysis that can extend your range of references and enlighten you about aspects of yourself. There is so much to learn from other people. This attentiveness leads to deep levels of appreciation of, and identification with, what lies under the surface. Observational study is capable of offering up valuable imagery that can unlock reserves of creativity in all theatre-makers. There are aesthetic qualities too, attached to the kind of observational analysis that helps us see people, places and things, even whole stories, in terms of their pattern and rhythm, their texture and contrast, perspective, structure and balance. These are dramatic and structural devices as well as artistic ones.

Much of the process of self-discovery lies well beyond the scope of any Movement course, but it can help. Postural habits, degrees of tension and recurring patterns of body gestures soon become clear as we observe ourselves in a variety of circumstances. More subtle and therefore more difficult to discern, being the result of years of use, are the colours and flavours of our dynamic range. Of the eight classifications of Laban's movement efforts—press, punch, flick, slash, dab, glide, float and wring—no more than four comprise the dynamic range of most of us. Unless you exercise and experiment with dynamic qualities beyond your accustomed use, you will feel, and probably look, unconvincing when the need arises to employ a different physicality.

Keith was always there, always present. With him it was about the doing rather than a reflective thing. I think you can get into bad habits at drama school because you can get so caught up in the theorising of a role, or theorising an approach to a role, that procrastination ends up just compounding you into something that isn't actually telling the story or that isn't useful.

NATHANIEL DEAN

The mind-body connection

The evidence for this interaction is irrefutable and universal. The mind and the body are inseparable. In fact it can be claimed that the body itself is a thinking organism. Of course it is possible to inhibit and interfere with its response, but the body reacts and reveals our emotional states and the workings of our mind. Since my early training with Bodenwieser it has also been my belief that the corollary is equally true: Every shaping of the body, every gesture, space use, change of focus or dynamics, should have its own justification, its own meaning, and supply its own motivation and imagery.

If you accept the mind-body connection and see it as fundamental to organic acting, then you must also accept that movement is as deeply involved with all matters of thinking, sensing, feeling, intuiting and behaving as it is with all things physical.

A state of harmony, of mutual response, between mind and body is something to dream about. Connecting the two in an ideal balance, so that no one unit of the partnership overpowers or undermines the other, is a relatively uncommon achievement. For most of us, the reality is a range of minor triumphs, uneasy truces, hard-won battles and open warfare, depending on the compatibility of the message exchange between them. In this regard, some important principles need to be emphasised. Firstly, because the inner lives are unique to each of us, no two people will react in the same way when confronted with the same situation. This fact has great implications for the actor.

If a serious accident occurs in a crowded street, there will be as many responses to the tragedy as there are people present to witness it. One of the bystanders will take charge immediately and purposefully, another may help but only after hesitating to reason with himself, a third will escape the scene and its responsibilities as fast as they can go, while another might faint or break down; and a fifth push

He pushed us to be intelligent, deliberate and aware of how we did anything. The aim was to gain understanding that movement always means something to an audience.
CHRIS STOLLERY

His understanding of theatre was quite extraordinary. He would say wonderful things like, 'Your voice isn't quite in your body yet,' or, 'Your body is ahead of your mind.'

WENDY STREHLOW

their way to the front of the crowd to get a better view. However, you are not always at the mercy of the impulses and reactions occasioned by unforeseen circumstances. More frequently, as you approach occasions of consequence (an audition, an interview, a business convention or a class) for which the prevailing conditions can be anticipated, you can plan the modifications to your manner and behaviour appropriately.

Body brain and body memory

The value of both of these to you as a performer is inestimable, not only in terms of truthful and spontaneous response to impulse and the moment, but in originality, creativity, quick learning and physical recall. Of course, this is a restatement of the mind-body interaction, but expressed in this way it can give a clearer understanding to the phenomenon. It is common knowledge that the movements we humans make are in response to messages from the brain. These are conducted to the appropriate muscle groups via the spinal cord, in response to the information transmitted to the brain by the network of the nervous system. All this is such a swift, unified and immediate negotiation of body and mind that we are unaware of the process we experience within our own bodies. Nor do we often observe it in the actions and reactions of other people.

In 'normal' circumstances, the double process of body-to-the-brain and brain-to-the-muscle is experienced as a single transaction, as if the hand that withdrew from the flame had itself a brain. It can appear as if the laugh muscles themselves had heard the joke and the brain had the sense of humour to appreciate it; and that the hand that stroked the puppy possessed its own heart and will. When you reach out to pull a friend from the path of a speeding vehicle, the feeling is more instinctive and body-oriented than conscious and brain-directed. In all of these reactions, the movements taken are of great complexity and involve fine judgments of distance, speed, strength, level, shape and dynamics, as well as the physical manifestations of the emotional state involved.

I recognise that in some circumstances the brain is more directly involved than the body and I am aware of the brain's decision-making function. I have experienced the brain's indecision, as though it needed time to make its choice of alternatives, saw more than one set of problems or was searching through old records for a similar situation. And there are other times when what I feel is the body doing the thinking. So often when I have been asked to solve a sudden creative problem, perhaps within an improvisation, and I have allowed my head-brain to inhibit the impulse of my body-brain, I have been disappointed with the unoriginal and un-spontaneous result. Conversely, there are occasions when the body deals with an unexpected occurrence so swiftly and accurately that the brain, in comparison to the wisdom and the quick thinking of the body-brain, has seemed taken aback by the body's inventiveness and can do no more than acknowledge what has taken place. I have had that experience when, as a choreographer, I surrendered so completely to my theme and to the images it evoked, to the music or the atmosphere I sought, that I could trust my body to create movement of much greater originality than my head could have devised. It is the totality of reaction and the truth of the spontaneous action that are so beautiful. Try responding to a great variety of situations, images, and instructions at a speed that gives no time for the head to take over. Instinct and impulse are too easily killed off when movement is the outcome of intellectualising.

'Head actor' is an expression that is used to describe the actor who must plan every movement he makes. He imposes this plan on his fellow actors without respect for, or reference to, what they are offering him; he anticipates the next moment instead of living within the present one; is lost and reduced when the circumstances of the performance vary from the rehearsal; and allows his brain to control the dramatic and physical presentation to the point that makes the work predictable, insensitive and unbelievable.

The brain is a spectacular repository of old memories, of things seen and done, of solutions already found. The body, however, when it is freed from inhibition and surrenders to the moment, is capable of the wit and ingenuity of an expert improviser and the freshness and originality of a good choreographer. As for the body memory, how could we expect to act well without it when we cannot get through our day-to-day lives without it? My body has memorised over the years an incredible number of insignificant tasks; and this leaves my mind (my front brain) available to plan my day, worry about my problems and cope with immediate realities. A task like shaving, once requiring total concentration to master, is now done for me so efficiently and unconsciously that most days I can't remember having done it. I achieve so much of my best thinking while driving the car. My front brain has such perfect confidence in my back brain driver that I am capable of conducting both activities, driving and thinking, simultaneously.

Strictly Ballroom: Catherine McClements and Baz Luhrmann, NIDA 1984. Photo from Sonia Todd's private collection.

You too, during a performance, while apparently engrossed with the text, the relationships, the intentions and so on, will also need to be dealing with technical problems of props, camera positions, lighting spots, dialect and costume and still be open to impulse and response to each fresh moment as the production unfolds. You need to repeat and repeat, for example, the lines of the text, till they are so known and justified that they can virtually be forgotten. Allowing them to emerge, as if spontaneously, from the back brain, leaving the front brain to take advantage of each fresh detail the circumstances of the performance provide. Similarly, in those theatre styles where more formal and technical movement is required—in sequences such as fights, dances, duels and mime—the greater the speed of learning and the more accurate the execution of the movement detail, the better. Body learning needs repetition, often more than head learning. The body brain may take longer than the head to *know*, but its memory is generally longer and more reliable. Remember the old saying that one never forgets how to ride a bicycle? Don't be afraid to repeat, as if you fear the process might bore you. You aren't there to entertain yourself. Besides, no one ever learned anything by being told or shown only once or twice. Repetition need never be dull and is always capable of fresh development and added significance.

My greatest experience with a teacher was with Keith. Amidst all the wisdom that Keith passed down to his students, and the greatest technical education he gave us in Movement and dance, perhaps the single most important lesson I learnt from him was how to learn—and to never give up the pursuit of learning.

BAZ LUHRMANN

We can all relate stories of the difficulty and frustration of being expected to get our minds around a new theory, mastering a new gadget, repeating a new process or remembering a new routine. I can think of no moment of greater excitement than when I reach understanding or mastery—that thrill when a fresh idea, caught and held in the front brain, slips back into the back brain and is absorbed by the mind as comfortably as if it had been my idea in the first place; and when the movement, held in the brain as coming from someone else's invention, drops down into my muscles and nervous system to become a true part of me and no longer a memory test.

3

The 'Good' Student

Keith was one of the first people—and not just in Australia—who found a way to teach Movement that was useful to actors.

BETTY WILLIAMS

Movement is doing. Movement is action. Movement is physical and requires our bodies to do it. We can talk about it, watch other people do it, theorise and discuss its principles, but to learn it, to improve the way we do it, to be able to self-correct and become autonomous, our movement needs to be experienced from within, kinaesthetically. Since we are inside our own movement we had better learn to work from inside, through the feel of what we do and how we do it. The alternative is the dependence on someone telling us when we are wrong and then telling us what to do to make it right.

Studying Movement is about learning how to learn experientially. That charismatic dynamo, Martha Meyers, in her book *Science of Dance Training* puts it well:

The emphasis... is on developing kinaesthetic awareness through introspec-
tion, leading to physical re-education. Moreover the process is as much
*one of subjective learning as of processing objective information.**

In this kind of approach, there is no required outcome, no right or
wrong, just imaginative opportunities to experiment and experience.
You turn the studio into a laboratory, you try things out and see what
discoveries you can make. Make such moments pleasurable departures
from the more formal teaching you no doubt receive. You will need all
the help you can get to become well-aligned, capable of elegance and
lyricism, have a strong presence and sophistication—and the rest of the
positive qualities. But the majority of the characters you will come to
play will have less admirable attributes, most of which can be relished.
Widening your choices by becoming familiar with the feel of movement
outside your own experience is an effective starting point. Let yourself
feel what it is like to take on shapes and displacements other than
your own. Move these off-balance, misshapen and distorted discoveries
into dimensions of space you have never entered before. Give yourself
permission and opportunity to explore eccentricity and extremes of
energy, both strong and weak. Move yourself out of your familiar use
of speed and time, tension and relaxation. Dare to be ugly, inside and
out. Explore your capacity for menace, temper and vindictiveness.

Actors are their own medium. You will need to be as intimate with
it as painters are with the quality, colour and texture of their paint.
It is only through awareness that we gain such self-knowledge. Actors
know only too well how differently an audience or critic reads their work
from what they intended. An actor's kinaesthetic sense and discerning
observation of themselves, as well as a preparedness to consider advice
from informed sources, can help build that security of self-image needed
as a basis for the acting craft.

---

*   P M Clarkson & M Skrinar (eds), *Science of Dance Training*, Champaign, IL, Human Kinetics Books
1988

One of the most valuable results of this form of learning is in the prevention of injury. The movers who come to know the feel of correct body usage are those most capable of recognising when things are amiss and of feeling their way into the process of self-correction. It is the experiencing, not just the doing, of these states and actions that carries the value. It is important to allow yourself sufficient experimentation time with all these unfamiliar dynamics and sensations for you to be confident in engaging them when the time comes to play a character whose physicality and psychology is unlike your own.

Movement is also concerned with your own physical condition, your stamina, state of health, strength and self-discipline. Your tools are your voice and body, and the demands of a professional career require you to maintain a standard of fitness, energy and body confidence that will last a lifetime. Your physical awareness and body ownership should be such that it allows you to be seen as capable of a variety of roles and not trapped into a type-cast physicality that could limit your professional life.

Movement Courses

The varied backgrounds and lack of consistent approach of those who teach Movement has led to the subject called Movement for Actors being a different study from one academy to another. This means that, in many cases, actors are being taught something that could more accurately be described as 'movement that is a specific training for another skill or art form, but will hopefully be just as effective for actors'. In contrast, courses for acting, voice and improvisation are basically similar.

Through your study you will hopefully become as free as possible from the limiting effects of tension, mannerism, inhibition and the thousand other problem areas that restrict an actor. By applying yourself diligently you will also acquire the technical capacity to do what arises from your own imagination or those things that will be asked of you by a director, choreographer or Movement director. These last two pursuits are entirely different matters, and can become a very serious dichotomy for an actor. I have seen too many good instinctive actors, capable of thrillingly inventive contributions to a performance, fall to pieces when required to make the formal aspects of a production appear as spontaneous as those of their own devising. I am familiar, too, with those who can confidently bring fresh life to whatever movement or style is set for them, and yet they have only restricted access to an imaginative, personal movement style.

Your aim is to solve the problems of acting—that is, to physically reveal the full life of the characters you play, their background, temperament, needs, motivation, changing intentions and inner life, the relationships and the psychological details of a person's history. As an actor you have only your voice and your body, the author's words and your movement to convey all this and more. You need to understand and manipulate the elements of space, time and dynamics, to develop a body language that can reveal vulnerability, varying energies and appetites, and be accurately read by the audience. Within any Movement class, and beyond any physical skill you are acquiring you should also seek to develop emotional access and courage, spontaneous response to ideas and imagery, and skill in the collaborative aspects of acting in an ensemble.

Movement is a long process for even the most talented of learners. Its width and range is phenomenal. The theory can take years to absorb; no element of the subject is assimilated easily. Relating all the elements into a coordinated whole is equally painstaking. The sensory and the kinaesthetic experiences offered by a good course need time to be savoured and assessed. Experiments that lead to mature appreciation of the creative and imaginative processes can't be rushed if they are to lead to innovative work. It takes little time and trouble to find a competent, comfortable performance quality, and there are no shortcuts to developing a preferred way of linking voice and movement to acting, or fleshing out, an integrated personal method of role preparation.

Keith Bain teaching, Top Tote, NIDA 1986.

Collaborative skills don't happen overnight. Trust in yourself and others; the growth of emotional and physical courage and the breaking down of inhibitions are qualities that build gradually and can be killed off if rushed. Replacing limiting habits and mannerisms with more neutral ones that can bring range to an actor's expressiveness is no quick matter either. Time to think, to understand, to question, to see beyond, to feel, to imagine, to risk, to fail, to despair and recover, to yield up and yield to, are all part of the process. Combining the theoretical approaches of the subject with one's own responses to impulse and instinct is something else.

Beginnings

A study of Movement should firstly build respect for your body as the chief and irreplaceable instrument on which your career will depend. Secondly, gain an appreciation of its fragility and its strength. Thirdly, devise and establish a personal program of conditioning to maintain fitness and tone throughout your professional life; and fourthly, achieve a personal approach to characterisation and physicalisation based on those explorations which have led to the most imaginative and fitting ways of working in any medium.

Not everyone likes the physical qualities they have inherited or allowed to develop. I have too frequently seen actors preoccupied with weight, height, a particular body part, body proportion, colouring that is destructive to their self-image and progress. Too bad, I say. Some of these aspects are capable of change and improvement and you are a fool not to use your independent study and the classes to make those improvements. What can't be changed is best accepted and should not be allowed to produce an emotional or inhibiting response. The important thing is to make the most of those features that will remain distinctive all your life. I know many actors who have turned particular aspects of their body and voice that might have been obstacles, into a tool with which to forge a rewarding career.

Don't be too eager to confront yourself too suddenly with purely technical exercises, heavy theory, or activity that requires elaborate instruction. A fine starting point is simply to feel awareness, control and ownership of your body. Before you can be expected to move out of yourself and into the body-mind of other characters, or, conversely, absorb the concept of another character, you must know and own and have control over yourself.

I don't claim that studying Movement is a cure-all for our inadequacies. But a program that builds fundamental body qualities, plus mind preparations designed to animate and focus the totality of our powers in our personal and professional life, can be of immense benefit.

The 'ideal' student

The list that follows is a wish-list, made up mostly of what all trainee and experienced actors should do:

- allow yourself to be inspired, excited, curious, challenged and enthused.
- break down, clarify and integrate the information you are receiving.
- make clear the aims and objectives, define the qualities demanded by the given circumstances.
- examine, diagnose, assess and cure.
- encourage yourself to be a brave learner and performer.

All this is not as simple as it sounds. Any system in any profession that depends on asking the right questions of ourselves is always problematic. But it produces a technique based on self-knowledge that is invaluable. I believe that studying the craft should lead not to a formula or a collection of recipes for acting. You should strive to create your own method from the discoveries made during classwork, rehearsal and performance; and the experiences you have gained through exploring the options and theoretical approaches.

Know your own industry

It is important to have knowledge of the history of theatre, the fine arts, and an informed interest in film and television.

It always comes as a surprise to discover how many professionals are content to be simple practitioners of their art form, incurious about its historical and philosophical dimensions, let alone its relationship to other branches of the arts. I know quite a few teachers of the arts who seldom, if ever, attend dance performances, concerts, operas or musicals, never visit galleries and exhibitions and infrequently keep up with films and plays. In fact, dance, music, theatre and the visual arts are all richly interdependent. I can't claim that a dancer would necessarily leap higher and spin faster by appreciating the traditions from which the choreographer and composer came, but I do claim that those leaps and spins could be invested with a sense of purpose and a confidence of style when danced by someone for whom the background is as significant as the technique. As a learner I had very few teachers who took the time and care to place the practical work I was doing

Keith Bain, *Central Australian Suite,* ABC TV 1957.

into an artistic context, but those who did personalised my study by recounting episodes from their own backgrounds, cross-referenced study with relevant events, times, people and places and lit up corners of the arts world in a way that has informed and inspired me ever since.

Even if you are no expert on the history and interconnections of the fine arts, you should at least be aware of the current state of the branch of the performing arts which you are preparing to enter. In drama that would entail a keen interest in the seasons of local and national companies, what kind of repertoire they choose, who the privileged actors are, who is directing what, and the latest scripts and writers.

You will also be working with people operating in related fields. Designers and lighting experts are good examples. They are visual artists who must be dramatically aware and theatrically knowledgeable to serve as artistic partners in the collaborative act of making theatre. But I fear many of our directors and our actors remain accidental and uninformed visual artists, even though they may reveal an intuitive skill. The director, as spectator, creator and judge of the work of his cast, is in a better position than the actor to assess his success in integrating the performing, dramaturgical and visual potential of his production. The actor cannot stand outside his work and judge it in relation to the rest of the company, the script and the audience. In visual terms, the actor is painting a picture that he alone cannot see.

Learn to teach yourself

I would urge you also to extend the references that give additional dimension to your chosen study. They could be literary, aesthetic, historical, political, environmental; they could include current affairs, social issues, matters of spirituality; they certainly should involve career management, the pattern of existing companies, their directors and the company philosophies, the range of performing styles and what is happening in the field both here and abroad. These things are fodder for your artistic imagination; they give perspective to your professional decision-making and context for everything you encounter. Not for a minute am I suggesting you should devote yourself to being an expert; but capturing the odd anecdote, a special memory, engaging in a chat about a recent film or novel, making a comparison between the work in progress and a topical or historical occasion, can enrich the learning process by raising questions and awakening curiosity.

It is very easy to connect with women about their bodies. But men, they don't want to know. Yet Keith gets right in there and he gets to the depth of the men and the boys that he teaches.
ROBINA BEARD

I like the distinction between surface and deep approaches to learning. Surface learning may lead to a capacity to reproduce what the teacher wants, but it will be without an understanding of the work's significance or appreciation of its relevance to the field of study. That comes from actively participating in discussion and therefore gaining the freedom to direct your own work and progress. As a student don't become a passive object that is simply told what to do and how to do it, who is criticised for not doing it. Use your own in-built faculties to sense your own problems and seek out your own solutions. It is recognition and connection that lead to deep learning.

Maintain a sense of the whole person and the whole subject in your learning

Naturally, in any class, a teacher can teach only one aspect of the subject at a time. Thus the teacher can direct attention to only certain aspects of you, the student, at any one time. The sad implication behind an expression such as 'having your voice trained', is that this process involves only the vocal chords. Singing training largely consists of years spent standing formally beside a piano in a box-like studio, and giving prolonged inward focus on the placement of breath, articulation, tone and so on. Then, after essentially being reduced to a sound-producing mechanism, the singer is expected to perform onstage with freedom and ease; to be open to impulse, remain un-selfconscious in action, be sensitive to character and, with technique successfully hidden, present as an artistically-whole human being. Dance teachers, similarly, are frequently guilty of teaching legs, feet, arms and all the anatomical bits rather than the whole dancer. Worse, whenever the emphasis is placed solely on the technical and physical, critical aspects of the individual are not just being neglected, they are being destroyed. In any one day at drama school, a student can be split by the timetable and the teaching into being a body at one moment, a voice at another, then a brain and, with luck, an imagination.

In acquiring a technique for mastery in any area of activity, of course there is a need to focus on isolated details and specific actions. The complexity of a human being and the diversity of subjects means that to examine the whole at once is out of the question. So you need to find a way to reassemble what the technical demands separate. Try to see not only the fact that the bits relate to the whole but experience *how* the bits *become* the whole. This task of construction can be even more difficult than learning each separate skill or revelation in the first place. When confronted with new work in its fullest form, you first need to break down what is being introduced, element by element, to allow for the repetition that learning requires, and then for the elements to be given their significance and emphasis.

Respect the individuality of your response to the learning process

No two people are born with the same gifts and abilities; nor do they learn at the same speed, have the same powers of concentration, respond equally to the same instruction or find the same ease or pleasure in class and performance. We all differ in our natural talents, our temperament and our capacity to acquire technique. If these facts are ignored, then you will be causing yourself problems, not solving them. In the training of any of the artistic disciplines, it is important that you give yourself permission first to discover, and then come to terms with, your individual rate of learning.

The big lesson you learn through Keith is standing on your own two feet. If you are going to make a bold choice, make it wisely and make it really outrageous and do it by yourself. Don't be reliant on anyone.

NATHANIEL DEAN

We can all recall how easily we understood those studies for which we seemed to have the right body and brain, and how mysterious others remained. With self-awareness you can learn whether a problem is due to laziness, self-image or fear of failure, and devise a way of dealing with each case. You may have a tendency to pick up new material quickly yet not retain or extend it. You may be slow to grasp and absorb, but having done so will have learned it forever. Remember, the last thing you need to become is self-destructive, competitive or despairing, or to see yourself as slow or unimaginative through comparing yourself with others. How to come to terms with discovered strengths and weaknesses, and how to avoid emotional surrender, are two of the greatest lessons a budding artist can learn.

Start from what is most basic. Start from what you know.

In studying Movement, I have found no activity more helpful to use as a starting point than walking, in all its variations and with all its associated extensions, including running, stopping, starting, changing speed and direction. It is a fabulous and safe warm-up. It leads to an infinite range of explorations involving space, time, weight, energy, focus and postural variations. It makes clear all the elementary principles of alignment: opposition, gravity control, balance, economy and neutrality and mind-body connection; it reveals mannerism; encourages grounded-ness and the use of peripheral vision; and it inhibits nobody.

It can be made to include meetings and departures, the contrasts of moving in the same way as others and of being different and separate. The walks can be aimless or towards objectives. They can be escapes and chases with all the accompanying emotional states. They can amble, march, stumble and stagger, dart and dodge.

Cultivate your creativity

Maintain a sense of play in all explorations in Movement. There's nothing like fun and laughter to free up and animate the whole mechanism

He had a profound impact on the way I conducted myself physically, in particular the matter of getting me out of my body and standing at full height. This may seem like a simple thing, but our bodies being the black box flight recorders of all the emotional, physical and spiritual travels undertaken, are often locked tight, as mine certainly was... I remember walking down Cleveland Street after almost a year's work with Keith and having to stop as I had the feeling that I had forgotten how to walk. So in that sense, our work with Keith went to a very deep level, in my case literally learning how to walk again. Every day of my life I self-correct my posture, probably at least 30 times a day, still pulling out of myself.

RICHARD ROXBURGH

and set the imagination afire. By this I mean not just fun as in pleasure in moving, but physical jokes and silliness—quirky, absurd, witty, bold, crude, rude, pompous, over-the-top stuff. If theatre is to grow, change, adapt and diversify, it needs theatre artists with ideas, strong views and passions, and the capacity to give theatrical form to them in the creation of innovative work.

Creativity includes an understanding of basic aesthetic principles and an awareness of fundamental compositional techniques, plus lots of time and opportunity to play creative games. Imagination and creativity need exercising as much as our other capacities. Time must be devoted to appreciating concepts of form, spatial balance, contrasts in dynamics, energy levels; in establishing focus, building to climax and finding the image and symbol behind the facts on which the composition is based. All these and such elements of composition as symmetry, asymmetry, unison, canon, dramatic as well as random rhythms, speed and timing don't require detailed theorising. They can be easily experienced and made functional by game playing, improvisation on a variety of themes and simple problem-solving experiments. Encourage yourself to be sensitive to design, levels, transitions, moments of change, wit and humour as a dramatic tool, degrees of stylisation and the dramatic potential of body shapes and paths in space.

Well-structured improvisation can develop amazing facility for spontaneous experiments in movement, based on impulse, moods and relationships. The empowerment of the modern actor and dancer to make suggestions, offer choices, exercise artistic judgment and experiment with artistic possibilities—to be a creative collaborator—is both important and exciting.

The functions of actor and director have changed radically since my early years in professional theatre. I remember the practice of 'blocking' by which the director dictated virtually every move, every bit of business, even every vocal inflection, while the actor strove to find dramatic justification for all of this and, at the same time reveal a degree of spontaneity. The stage picture was all important. I can recall the search for the perfect spot and angle, the perfect pause and suspended gesture. Happily, directions like: 'Just ease an inch stage left, dear. Not too much. Back a little bit. That's better. We'll keep that', are rarely heard today. I remember the actors noting the details in their scripts, to ensure the blocking would remain fixed throughout the run of the show. Many a rehearsal came to a stop while the actors argued whether one of them should have crossed from upstage centre to downstage prompt in front of, or behind, the table. I recall, too, the relief and excitement in the rehearsal process on the day when the blocking was done.

The change to wider creative input from the cast, whilst the director edits the actors' offerings, has altered the process greatly. It has also demanded from actors a higher standard of creative artistry that must be prepared for. Moreover, the overcrowded condition of the profession is not likely to diminish, so you will need enough skill to keep your place as both a creative collaborator and a theatre maker, and have the confidence to initiate work of your own.

Be open to the imagery and motivation used in both the learning and creative processes

Most teachers, directors and choreographers find images to denote dynamic responses, to add colour and quality to characterisations and relationships and to give depth and dimension to otherwise unremarkable dramatic realisations. All the intellectualising, analysis and technical descriptions in the world can fail to release the spark that is essential to

*I remember watching class first. I was
so impressed by the way he described
movement—not just how to do it, but
how you feel. More about taking care
of it internally. As soon as I joined
those classes I felt that feeling of joy
of moving. He'd stand there and spend
five minutes smelling the air and getting
all of us to create an image in front
of us of where we wanted to go. And
we'd set up that image before we even
started. His imagery was just amazing.
I still use it for teaching today.*

RUTH OSBORNE

the mastery of a movement or a moment. Yet a single image conjured from a most surprising source can trigger off impulses and understandings that lead to the revelations which had been so evasive. Clever imagery can solve the problems of external qualities like body shape, speed, paths of direction, gesture patterns and details of mannerism. Insightful images can be absorbed into the inner life, into mind, guts, heart and essence, and work outwards from there to the level of physicality desired. The best images spark a transformational effect by connecting the inner and outer aspects and linking us more fully to the other actors, to the theme of the piece, and its setting.

Good images somehow bypass the grinding wheels of the fact-loving brain, and find their way more directly to the imaginative centre within us. Visceral, physical, kinaesthetic and muscular impulses seem to rise immediately from that centre, leading to more spontaneous responses than are likely to result from an intellectual process. Apart from their help in the actual acting processes, certain images can also still the distracting patterns of the mind and engender sensations of well-being, inner calm and centeredness.

Figurative language works for so many aspects of a performer's life. The metaphors that express our own and other people's lives determine an artistic uniqueness. All the bare facts of living and being are translatable into imagery that can in turn become the stuff of the magic that is theatre. Turning fact into imagery, or finding the imagery behind the fact, is one of the most important features of the concept of transformation. It is the image perceived and felt beyond the facts that gives universality to those facts, allowing us to connect with the stories, the predicaments, doubts and uncertainties of others as if they were our own. Stanislavski's great 'what if' offers us a way to richer imagery, if it is agreed that the definition of an image includes the idea of it being a mental picture and a concept of people, places and events. The directors and performers whose work I most admire have the judgment to surround the basic facts of a production with a concept that gives a point of view and a field of reference and keeps the two in perfect balance.

Beware 'the facts'

Facts are great food for the brain. Facts give information and no performer can have too much of that. But information will be no more than baggage unless it leads to a physical realisation. After all, acting is the doing of the intellectual content. It is the manifestation, and it is this that the audience sees and hears. I often marvel at the researched information that performers and creators talk to me about—all the themes, sub-plots and subtleties of the promised play, ballet or film. Then I see the work and wonder what had happened to all their talk. So little from their analysis of the text had emerged in their playing—things like temperament, social standing, psychological complexities, prejudices, failings, education, relationships, ambitions. Every fact is a problem for you to solve; your character's age, occupation, relationships, positive and negative qualities are all facts. Not every fact easily suggests the way to play it, to move it and give evidence of its existence. This is where I believe imagery comes in again. A fact can sit in your brain like a bird in a cage, but a well-chosen image arising from that fact can set up an empathetic response, a muscular stirring, a dynamic and a sensory adjustment that brings it out into the light.

If I set out to help you improve your body alignment by means of scientifically-based instruction, I would probably begin by having you stand still and then assist in adjusting the body parts individually to make you aware of the anatomical process. But when I take stock of the finished posture I might well find that the line is perfect but I have robbed you of all potential and motivation for new movement. I had emptied you of your sense of normality and personality and replaced

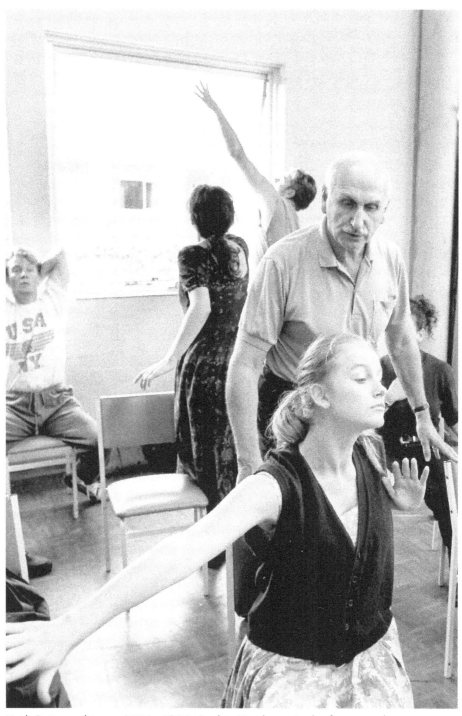

Keith Bain teaching at NIDA, 1994, Sophie Heathcote in the foreground.

your extrovert focus, and interest in the world, with an introverted state of being—in fact reduced you to a mere geometric entity.

If, on the other hand, I gave you an active image that would keep you walking with purpose and intention, toss in some images to add to the release of your energy and sense of self, such as extending your aerial, turning on your headlights, walking away from the camera, claiming your real height, floating your head, opening up your peripheral vision by seeing the world around you on the wide screen, I will have achieved an improved alignment. I will also have increased your sense of presence, animated your energy centres, awakened your five senses, alerted you to a new spatial awareness and added to your powers of transmission and reception.

Generally speaking, my preferred images are those that tend to recall old experiences, old sensory and emotional memories. But without the critical faculty of judgment, a solution to any problem is likely to cause another problem—like some medicines have their side effects. I will never forget how I once felt when given a movement assignment based on an image that did more to insult my intelligence than exercise my imagination muscles. I also remember a spine-roll exercise being excellently explained by a teacher new to me, which kept me confident and involved until the moment when, with my head somewhere down near my ankles, my bum in the air and my backbone in a fantastic curve, I heard her asking me to imagine melted chocolate dripping down from my tailbone to a point on the floor between my heels. I felt as absurd as if it was actually happening and everyone around me was enjoying the spectacle.

Teachers and directors need judgment in the images that they offer. In mentioning a tiger, they might find themselves confronted with the full beast in all its terror and magnificence when all the image was intended to conjure was a well-oiled walk or an unpredictable ambivalence. Performers, too, need care in assimilating an image into their work process so that what is released into the performance is no more than a specific element of its essence, an aspect of its potential—a flavour, a hint, a mere whiff and not, say, the actual animal.

Things that Keith said really stuck with you. He said: 'Just imagine your sternum, in the middle of your breastbone, as a large headlight beaming out'... a car headlamp. Such a great image. It's not only just to keep your back straight, but it's also to beam out the whole performance, rather than just doing it through your head, your brain... It's engaging the body, the physicality of the whole performance.

KERRY WALKER

Actors, generally speaking, are energetic, generous and over-ready to let it all out and go the full distance. They are more inclined to let fly with the emotional states than play against them. They are more tempted to turn up the volume than explore the controls that people impose on themselves in life. They find it hard to resist telling their audience too much at one time. The bigness of little movement and the concept that *less is more* do not hold the same fascination as *go for your life*.

The same goes for the application of theoretical principles to the acting process. Take the eight categories of movement efforts as analysed by Laban—press, punch, flick, slash, dab, glide, float and wring. These are virtual images which in themselves can lead to an excess of externalised and distracting business when a subtle reduction or increase in tension, a slight readjustment of the body weight, a psychological adjustment, a more telling gesture pattern or a changed light in the eye would have been sufficient. More often than not, the sensation of the potential of the wring or the float or the press will be enough to bring about the desired flavour in the body and the voice.

All aspects of Movement can be improved

Not for a minute do I believe that each of us can be taught to succeed in everything we undertake. Minds that can comprehend and be excited by certain fields of study will fail to absorb a range of others; bodies that respond with ease and style in one activity will remain defeated by another. However, the most inflexible body can be loosened to a degree; rhythmic response can be improved; the uncoordinated and the poorly aligned are easily helped; slow learning can be speeded up; dynamic range can be extended; observational analysis can be sharpened, inhibitions reduced, tensions freed, body memory made more reliable and physical courage increased.

I often marvel at how contradictory and unpredictable each person's parcel of natural gifts proves to be. A sportsman and gymnast, born to run, jump, throw, fly through the air, judge distance and sense time, can be discovered to move awkwardly and lack coordination in an activity like dance or mime. I have seen highly-skilled dancers whose timing and coordination in their own field are miraculous, but who are helpless at catching or hitting a ball. In fact, many dancers cannot move easily even from one form of dance to another. I watch skateboard and surfboard riders who perform manoeuvres of virtuosic technique; but are incapable of transferring them to any other medium.

It is all very well to acknowledge and accept what we do not find easy to accomplish; but it is a great deal better to seek strategies that might narrow the gaps and strengthen the weaknesses. This task becomes even more monumental when we realise how complex its elements are. In any student those differences in ability, and capacity to learn, could be genetically based. Or they could be the result of acquired prejudices that close the mind or view certain areas of movement with disdain or fear. These people are certainly affected by their private image of themselves and the way they have come to see themselves in relation to others. Temperament also plays an important part in an actor's capacity for self-discipline, nervous energy, sensitivity. Ambition and motivation are also big factors.

Problems require solutions

All too often I hear dance teachers in class highlighting a student's problems with negative comments, as if repeated reminders that they are off the beat will bring about a cure. Movement teachers are similarly guilty of critical remarks—about a young actor's spatial insensitivity, for instance— that offer no constructive clue to how this might be overcome. A student who responds over-emotionally to a difficulty is likely to produce only negative results because it exaggerates the problem and encourages self-castigation. It is important, instead, to face the difficulty as a simple fact, one to be given a priority but not allowed to become a block to progress, a cause of inhibition or self-doubt.

Cultivate the capacity to assess progress, diagnose difficulties and pin-point problems of temperament and technique

None of this is as easy as it sounds. And it is worth remembering that some of the best learning is done retrospectively. Find time to reflect and analyse. For example, at the end of a lesson give yourself a quick rundown of the scope and focus of the class, one that also allows you to review what has or has not been clear to you, what has been achieved and where the main points of significance lie. This will lead to self-assessment, whereby you can discover a basis for evaluating your own progress.

The truth is that the majority of us are too often faced with evidence that this body of ours is far from being under our ownership and control. Its limitations deny us, leaving us disappointed in what we have achieved compared with what we intended. We cannot depend on it to function consistently well. We are embarrassed by its lapses into clumsiness and restricted by its lack of versatility. It frustrates us by its failure to learn new things accurately and quickly. It can give away secrets we are anxious to conceal and block impulses that would express the truth. Its tensions, when evident in the outer body, can block both the transmission of our inner qualities and information received from outside. Assessment, however, requires more than the listing of deficiencies and shortcomings. It is not just criticism. You will be frustrated, disappointed, even a little angry with yourself and very self-conscious; but in retrospect, away from the heat of the moment, you will have the opportunity to monitor

Keith was choreographing a production of Kalman's Countess Maritza *for Opera Australia. I thought I was pretty good one day when we were rehearsing a czardas with a high kick in it, so I said to Keith: 'Gosh, I got it right that time. I wasn't bad, was I?' And he said: 'That was nearly nice.'*
ROBERT GARD

your learning in an objective way. This capacity is a gift to possess, and a disadvantage not to possess. But beware, you will probably also be much more aware of your weaknesses than your strengths. Weaknesses can be very obvious. Most of the students I encounter are less sure of, and therefore less confident about, their strong points. On the other hand one of the greatest weaknesses can be giving yourself credit for strengths you don't possess. To counteract this, be aware of times when you are being confirmed in the things you do well, and open to the advice that is offered, regarding the qualities and understanding that is developing.

The process of self-assessment is where you learn to use the language of Movement, and find new words for things for which the majority of people have no means of expression—the sensations, the subtleties and flavours, the accompanying feelings and thought processes, the mind-body connections, the changes in intensity, the discrimination between strain and ease, between effort and economy. We shall probably never have the opportunity in our social life to talk about these precious things. When did you last sit down with an old pal and have a good heart-to-heart about your growing command of space, your sensitivity to timings and speeds, your powers of focus, your reducing self-consciousness?

But if we don't talk about them, we reach a point where we can't talk about them, and so they drift from our consciousness. It is both rare and liberating to be equally sensitive to what is happening within you, and because of you, and in relation to you.

The teacher's perspective

The formal class

The formal class works best for formal material and for basic techniques that apply equally to all members of the group. It gives the advantage of placing focus on the teacher, on demonstrations and instructions.

It also puts the teacher in the best position to observe those who need help, or encouragement. It allows each pupil to concentrate closely on solving the problem set, and it is an effective set-up for supervision and discipline. But it has its dangers. Students can easily hide or be hidden behind others if the class is large. In no time at all they will settle into the spot in the studio, or at the *barre*, they chose originally. I am sure there are long-term students who have taken the same position in class year after year and who have never faced any but the one wall throughout their entire training period.

For ten years I observed Keith's weekly class with NIDA first-year actors. Keith would work with the students in many different ways. Mostly he would start the class with students walking in a circle bringing their focus and attention to themselves. He would then get them to move across and through the space turning their awareness to their surroundings—this would develop by adding interaction with the other students. Keith would guide them, adding just a word or suggestion, taking them deeper into their exploration, always leaving them plenty of space for their own interpretation. This exploration of space could extend for some time but Keith was adept at judging when to change direction. Once they were totally engrossed he would simply say 'Drop that' and move on to something else—relaxation techniques, focus and balancing or rhythmic exercises, co-ordination—a variety of possibilities but often very practical exercises. The students, having a deeper level of concentration, were now able to absorb the information better. Sometimes Keith would get the students to sit on chairs in a semi-circle facing him and do focus, hand or back exercises. Other times he would teach social and ballroom dances; with the many patterns and sequences to learn and partnering techniques. This made for a very different dynamic in the classroom, one which Keith made endlessly enjoyable—there was the thrill of *Strictly Ballroom* and the Trocadero somewhere in the room!

By this time students were confident enough to enter the imaginary worlds they could create in Keith's classes. He had the ability to simultaneously build security and trust and as a consequence, great freedom in the classroom. There was a strong sense of building not only the students' physical capabilities and confidence but also their understanding and appreciation of how the Movement work informed their acting. The classes were both informative and fun!

It was not only what Keith taught but more importantly the way he taught. He engendered in students a belief in themselves, that they were capable of great things. He allowed them to extend themselves and expand their sense of potential. It was Keith's way with words, just the right phrase at the right moment. Countless times I saw the lights go on in a student's eyes and the revelations were great to behold. Another characteristic was how at the end of class Keith would always have an encouraging word for each student. He had the ability to work with a large group in a class and at the same time make each individual student feel special.

JULIA COTTON

The workshop

The workshop is an ideal alternative to the class for intensive and exploratory investigation into specific aspects of the course. Workshops might concentrate on particular techniques like mask work or circus skills, or be used when process rather than product is the aim of the lesson. Typically, a workshop allows experiment, evaluation, discussion, and freedom to fail or try another way. It achieves most when the atmosphere is supportive and encourages daring, and the teacher is more of a facilitator and encouraging guide than a sage authority figure.

The biggest hurdle to clear can be in setting up the focus of the workshop theme, firing up the energy and enthusiasm needed to propel the activity, then creating the atmosphere needed for the activity to remain productive and uninhibited. The tutors who handle this situation best express the objectives graphically in language that clarifies the ideas, animates the imagination and liberates the more inhibited students. Instructions need to be crystal clear, unclouded by over-explanation. After all, you are asking the group to dare to contribute their thoughts and feelings and you trust they will yield up possibilities none of you had visualised in advance. If individuals in the group are confused about the idea being investigated, you will have little hope of collaboration or teamwork.

Workshopping is a laboratory situation; it is about trial and error, unknown and unexpected outcomes, not certainties and end-results. It is the customary approach for developing self- or group-devised theatre pieces. You can workshop a theme to investigate its aptness as an idea for a new work. You can workshop an untried script, put it on the operating table and test its structure, strengths and shortcomings. You can test the appropriateness of a process of working: for example a choreographer or director keen to validate an unfamiliar way of creating. It is a wonderful, playful way to judge how far one can travel from, say, naturalism to the limits of stylisation. When handled well by a sensitive teacher it can lead students to an appreciation of, and skill in, the difficult practice of unselfish collaboration.

The master class

The master class is different again. Here the master, who is an expert on the subject, evaluates the one-at-a-time performance or presentation of individuals within that group, to the enlightenment of everyone present. All teaching requires sensitivity but this situation especially so. It should not be a platform for the master to show off, but there may be discreetly judged moments of demonstration to illustrate subtle phrasing, accent, rhythm, dynamics or technique. I love the practical opportunity a master class gives to get into precious discussion of the finer points of technique and performance. Unlike the general class, where certain specifics must often be overlooked so that all the class members may progress, the master class gives the master freedom to be philosophic and idealistic, to promote artistic and aesthetic viewpoints and to reinforce the highest principles of professional practice. It provides the perfect forum in which to lead an individual to make changes in a constructive fashion and for the benefit of all.

My favourite use of the master class is when the accent is on the students' creativity. Keen to encourage original and personal responses, I set a task for the second-year NIDA students which asked them to create a piece of theatre that was virtually a self–portrait, revealed through movement. The best of them were some of the bravest, most honest and original theatre pieces I have ever witnessed.

This project had arisen from my search for ways to exercise students' creativity through movement. The first tasks I set were based on character studies from the plays they were about to perform. Unsatisfied, I then experimented with offering them their own choice of themes from literature, art, the daily news and so on. What I began to observe was a special quality, a new depth and a passionate honesty that was present whenever the chosen theme involved some personal investment. The idea then dawned on me that their own lives—the ups and downs, the influences, the enthusiasms, the dreams and the wonders, rather than the imaginary lives of imaginary characters—were treasure troves of real memories, emotions and happenings that did not have to be guessed or pretended, only recalled.

Beyond simply an exercise in creativity the *movement pieces,* as we called them, were an opportunity for the students to see the dramatic resources of which they themselves were composed. I wanted them to look their inner life squarely in the eye. I wanted them to realise that, by their present age (late teens and early twenties) there was no emotional state they hadn't experienced to a rich degree. Most of all I wanted them to give dramatic form to their case histories by seeing the images behind the facts, while ruthlessly editing and shaping their story.

Noni Hazlehurst and Geoffrey Rush in *On Our Selection*. Dir George Whaley, Chor. Keith Bain, Jane St Theatre 1979.

On the value of the Movement pieces: Creative terror is a very good thing to experience. Wrestling with it becomes part of how you move and what you present. It's you in confrontation with your own worries or your own inadequacies that becomes the substance of the piece.
GEOFFREY RUSH

The second-year Movement piece shows that Keith understands that until you know where you are coming from or what drives you as a person and a performer, you will never be in control of what you do.
ANNA VOLSKA

To complete the task they were asked to create the set and choose the props that would best accommodate their chosen story, and a soundscape that would provide the atmospheres and references. They were encouraged to be brave in their uses of time and space, to go beyond the natural and the literal to deepen the truth of their statements, to put their fullest range of physical skills to the service of their artistic aims, to find transitions that were as telling as the contrasting sections that they joined, to experiment with irony and humour as well as dramatic techniques and not to be afraid to underplay, overplay, confront, uncover and tell it like it was.

The performance of the *Movement pieces* became the focus of a master class as each student in turn presented his or her work to the whole group, introducing it with relevant accounts of their intention and their process. Then it became my task to evaluate what we had seen, noting the strengths and the cleverness, analysing the structure, the imagery, the performance values and the impact, and offering alternative choices and refinements. The most profitable part of the exercise was often when the rest of the group offered up their reactions, giving credit to the originality and daring of the work and discussing big questions like, 'How many forms can theatre take?'

'How possible is it to break new ground?' 'How many ways can the truth be told?'

This kind of project should only be attempted when the course has advanced to the point where space games have been played, timing and rhythm have been investigated, skills have granted range and safety, a gamut of dynamic possibilities have been experienced and less ambitious and shorter phrases of movement have been tried.

The three T's

In my teaching I use very simple criteria for assessing students that I call the three Ts:

TALENT—that with which we are born. And a given as each of the students had succeeded through the rigorous audition process.

TECHNIQUE—that which we learn and develop. Levels of technical ability vary but I assess a student's ability to learn the skills and techniques provided in class. An ability to learn the craft enhances the student's talent and will prepare them for the practical requirements of the industry.

TEMPERAMENT—the manner in which we deal with challenges. This is a tricky one—no matter how talented a student might be, if they are

Bitter Sweet, l to r: Rupert Burns, Lee James, David Whitney, Kevin Scully. Dir. Robin Lovejoy, Chor. Keith Bain, Parade Theatre, NIDA 1982.

It was Keith who taught us the Three Ts, talent, technique and temperament, and they are all equal. Same as unemployment, the audition and the performance. All three must be equal. You can't be better at auditioning than at turning up and giving the product. You must survive unemployment by remaining interested and constantly working. Your talent is what you're born with. It will be apparent to anyone but you must not rest on it. You must develop your skills and your technique constantly. But what Keith focussed on constantly was temperament. Don't always show everything. Don't turn the lights up a hundred per cent the first thing. Keep something to yourself. Keep a secret inside.

LEE JAMES

not temperamentally suited theirs could be a hard road. Temperament also refers to the ability to have a strong enough sense of oneself to be able to depart freely into different characters secure in the knowledge that they could always return to a grounded sense of self.

All three must be appreciated and nurtured and in balance for the performer to be well-rounded and creatively accessible. The ideal student arrives with talent, is open to learning and building on their technical skills and with an even enough temperament to cope with the uncertainty of an unpredictable career.

PART II
The Practice

4

Fundamental Qualities of Movement

To have had the privilege to be under Keith's tutelage
is to have had the opportunity to evolve from a messy
excitable adolescent into a focused excitable actor. Whilst
at NIDA every problem I encountered with a character
or scene, be it physical, psychological, emotional,
textual, I would bring to Keith and unfailingly he would
enable me to tackle and solve them in his classes.
My dialogue with Keith has never stopped. His teachings
are the foundation of my technique. His suggestions are my
notes to self and his deep generosity and passion are a true
inspiration, and always the last thought to cross my mind
before walking on stage or before 'action' is called is Keith's
exquisite metaphor, 'to turn my headlights on'.

CATE BLANCHETT

There are essential, movement-based qualities on which all styles, techniques and movement forms are built; and they underlie the strengths of the most accomplished actors. The majority of performing artists possess them all, but only to a degree. The important thing is how they can be made to work for us, to help us do things better.

Firstly, by simply identifying, naming and isolating the components of these qualities, we can objectify and make specific each part of the total fabric of this subjective study of Movement.

Then we can put them to use in a number of ways:

- They are measures of differentiation to be used to distinguish one character from another and each character from ourselves.
- They serve as a basis for observational analysis and understanding of the movement and behaviour of society in general and other people in particular.
- They become a checklist against which we can measure our own basic components in the task of enlarging the conception we have of ourselves.
- They are available as points of reference when researching a text.
- They are a source of detail to make characters multi-dimensional. They lead us to the heart of the matter and of the role.

So what are these qualities? You may not agree with my list below. You may have more appropriate qualities of your own. Indeed, I keep finding new ones; I argue regularly with myself when I try to prioritise them. But without a well-considered list of what should be the actor's basic technical equipment it is easy to overlook certain essential elements and overemphasise others. As a student your view of your journey is more likely to be better balanced if the list can act as a guide and reference. When your list puts more than one of these fundamental qualities into a category, it implies that the connection between them is as important as the individual element.

Corporeal Qualities

The qualities listed below relate to technical control and ownership of the body itself. They are key attributes for the actor whose body needs to be ready for the considerable physical demands of a long career. If Movement for Actors was primarily a matter of physical skills, this would be the most important category. But I don't believe that for a minute. When I watch students practising leg stretches, splits and backbends, in preference to the skills that are more vital to a theatre artist's needs, I wonder if this reflects their teacher's priorities. I regularly see physical flexibility listed in surveys of new students as the most desirable fundamental quality. I guess it is because this leads to measurable results for both teachers and students, in a way that subtler and more subjective qualities don't. I see students prepared to give hours to walking on their hands, standing on their heads and flying through the air—time that would be better spent on walking and standing on their own two feet, being grounded on the floor, in proper alignment and striving to master this list of essential corporeal qualities that will make them versatile and proficient as an actor.

1. Alignment: body placement and displacement, the neutral body;
2. Balance: gravity and weight control, the law of opposition;
3. Strength: stamina; aerobic fitness;
4. Coordination: isolation control;
5. Peripheral vision;
6. Relaxation: control of tension, economy of effort;
7. Flexibility: agility, stillness.

1. Alignment

Body displacement, the neutral body

There is no denying the importance of the look of an actor, his composure and his ease in both action and stillness, and especially the potential range and power that can be sensed when the body is open, readable and unselfconsciously aligned. The well-aligned body is in an ideal state for movement to begin. In a state of alignment the building blocks of the body are so perfectly stacked that no one part is taking the strain of another, and the skeleton, muscles and inner organs are freely available to function to their best advantage.

The well-aligned body places the performer in that pre-expressive state in which the life force is ready to be tapped. Poor alignment, especially when it results from dropping the weight of each body part down onto the one below, has the effect of killing off the potential expressiveness of important emotional centres and release points. When the back of the neck collapses and the chest, in turn, yields to the weight of the head and shoulders, the resulting death of the body centre drains the life out of the arms and hands and even the small muscles of the face, and with it the response to impulse. Conversely, good alignment and the neutral state allow the impulses that arise from our thinking, sensing and feeling to reach their fullest expression, and for them to be read by others explicitly and vividly.

Most of us, as the years pass, yield to some combination of over-relaxed slumps and over-tense displacements that become so habitual that they feel, and are accepted by us, as normal. The collapsed shapes of many elderly people are frequently the end product of poor alignment in their youth. I can often see in the bodies of young children the tragic shape of the old man or woman they will become. Alignment will help us avoid mannerisms, repetitive gesturing and recurring body shapes. Unless these are neutralised they are likely to be carried into performance regardless of the play or the character. It is a familiar sight to see certain actors representing all their characters in a similar way.

They complain of being type-cast without realising that their *in-character* physicality is so recognisable that it dictates their range of casting. If an actor already looks like a baddie, a victim or a best friend, who can blame the casting director for giving him the job?

Alignment not only grants us access to our best physical resources but is one of the main links between natural movement and the formal techniques of other physical studies. Alignment is an aid to coordination, enabling the body parts to function as a connected unit. It is basic to solving the difficulties of balance, turning, jumping and landing. It can be the key to aesthetic problems of style, line and the effective wearing of costume. Until alignment is secure, the body itself is at risk of strain and injury.

In an aligned and lengthened state, all parts of the body are fed equally from our central energy source. One of the joys of being alive is sensing the flow of power upwards, outwards, downwards, not only to all the body extremities, but beyond these and into the space around us. This projected dynamism constitutes much of our personal aura, our presence, our potential, our expressiveness. So essential is it that it needs to become habitual to the artist. It is a lot of work, but it is worth the effort to make the aligned state a habit. A habit is not a habit until it occurs unconsciously.

I am always being amazed by the big differences that result from tiny changes. The spine has only to slump a little and, in consequence, the chest hollows, the head protrudes, the shoulders drop forward; the arms will droop and the pelvis may tilt forward and upwards. When the spine is even slightly overarched the neck shows tension and the chest is forced forward. There will be greater width across the top of the chest than across the upper back, the shoulders will be pulled back and the upper arm locked to the shoulder so that gesturing may be limited to indirect flapping of the lower arm; the bottom will stick out and the pelvis tilt down towards the floor. Each displacement has its accompanying repercussions of shape, energy flow and dynamic range that change the location of the body's dynamic centre, as well as killing off or over-emphasising some of the release points and emotional centres of the body. Alignment is not hard to achieve, at least in physical terms. If you really want to make changes you can achieve results surprisingly quickly. Resistance can arise from self-satisfaction or lack of conviction about the values of the change, but often the main obstacle is self-image.

In assuming a new alignment, you must realise you are asking much more of yourself than simply rearranging a few body parts. Every detail of the way you stand, the mannerisms and inhibitions, the way you use space and time, all represent your personal statement to the world. You have become your own self-portrait—a wonderful, unique signature: it reveals the value you put on yourself and your true nature; it encapsulates your response to peer pressure and the fashions of your generation, and displays the masks that conceal some feelings and reveal others. Interference with what represents all that you think of yourself, your society and how others think of you, could be more than you dare to allow. Inner change can be painful, even frightening.

If each of us marked our position on a line, one end of which represented a single reaction or quality and the other end its opposite, it would be rare for most of us to mark our spot in the very centre of the range, which is where 'the neutral body' would be. For example, if one pole indicated the degree to which we yielded to our weight and the force of gravity, and the other the degree to which we resisted these factors, where would you belong and what might be the implications? Just as the neutral voice sits comfortably balanced between an over-articulated, highly accented quality and a slurred, lazy mumble, so the neutral body too, is at that position of balance between extremes.

I have tried to find alternatives to all the systems that encourage an introverted process to achieve an aligned state. By this I mean those systems that say: 'Tuck this bit under, widen that, lift something here and relax something there.' They seem to destroy all outward focus and potential for motivated movement. I have never been drawn to exercises that close off essential faculties and inner qualities simply in order to achieve physical ones. It is important to maintain the mind-body connection as constantly as possible, even in stretching or warm-up classes. For example, familiar exercises like sit-ups may well produce an effect of strength and stamina. But unless there is encouragement to add focus, gesture and varying dynamics we are simply reinforcing emptiness.

One process that produces postural results quickly is walking. For this exploration, I like to begin by walking the space, relaxed and informal—as if you had all the time in the world—and with as little sense of being observed as possible. That's the hard bit. Give yourself time to come to terms with, but not adjust to, your preferred speed and energy level. Notice habits that have developed. Such things as uneven arm swings, shuffling footwork, pockets of tension or over-relaxation, head and shoulder displacements, odd hip swings etc. Then while still walking, find your full height, not by force or exaggeration but simply by taking advantage of the body length that is there waiting to be called on. Then compare the many new sensations that this produces with what you were aware of before. The unfamiliarity of some of the changes can shock at first, as well as delight. Not just the outward and mechanical changes but especially the inner ones of body unity, fresh energy, awareness of interior spaces and an adjusted self-image. As you continue a pattern of changes from full height back to the original state, you can become increasingly conscious of old habits and the advantages of efficiency and facility that flow from lengthening the skeleton. Next, claim the space above yourself by *putting up your aerial* through the top of your skull as an extension of your newly-experienced length. Concerning yourself with this image usually frees you from an introverted, self-conscious state and can offer a taste of a burgeoning physical presence.

Following that, imagine you are walking away from a camera which is filming you from behind. You might never have given your back a moment's thought, yet to me, the back is capable of coping with a considerable percentage of the body's work. The back needs to be long, strong, wide, and trusted to be your body's frame and pride. It frees your limbs and allows your head to float upwards on the top of the neck. Other images work well for this same dimension: for girls, think of a light cloak flowing backwards from your shoulders as you walk, or a dress with a long, weighted train; and for boys. imagine wearing a cape.

A Cheery Soul: l to r Jan Hamilton, Robyn Nevin, Peter Carroll. Dir. Jim Sharman, Chor. Keith Bain, Sydney Theatre Company, 1979.

Having dealt with these extensions of spatial awareness, both above and behind you, open up your peripheral vision. This will give a stereoscopic view of the space you occupy. Without looking up or down you should be able to see, and therefore take into account and react to, all that is on the ceiling and on the floor in front, as well as out to both sides.

Finally, as you continue to walk, put your headlights on—huge beams of light emanating from you chest or your entire torso—and allow yourself to feel the accompanying sense of body focus, purpose, intention, destination and outgoing energy release. With all these images operating in unison you will have energised internally, sharpened the senses, felt your way into a greatly improved alignment and added to your presence and feelings of personal power. All this without having mentioned one body part.

You can put these images into practice in private or in the most public of environments, without fear of detection by unsuspecting shoppers and passing pedestrians. With repeated practice the body will begin to absorb the changes that follow and make them part of a new awareness.

2. Balance

Gravity control, the law of opposition

Posture and therefore alignment are fundamental elements of balance control, whether we are dealing with a complicated activity or the simplest. Every displacement of our body parts creates a potential problem of balance even if we are doing nothing more complicated than walking, stopping or turning around. Lifting and supporting another body, balancing on a narrow beam or riding a bicycle are typical of a great number of skills involving balance that actors could be asked to perform within certain productions. It is therefore advisable that balance becomes a technique rather than a lucky accident.

The wobble that accompanies most attempts to hold balance when standing on one leg, produces such an amount of action and adjustment of the torso, arms and head that it can look as if the problem lies in the upper body. On the contrary, the cause is more likely to be traced to a failure of control in the feet and the need to maintain equal pressure under the three points of the foot—the ball of the big toe, the ball of the little toe and the ball of the heel. When rising onto half point, on one or both feet, it is common to lose equal pressure under the balls of the little toe and the big toe, so that the body wobbles as the ankle loses its straightness and strength with each shift of weight from the outside to the inside edge of the foot. I hear people excuse their insecure balance by claiming that they have weak ankles, because they see and feel their ankles moving unsteadily under them. Equalise the inner and outer pressures and the ankle automatically holds its straightness.

Feet and ankles need lots of work. In most people the foot is that dead thing hanging on the end of their leg, handy enough to land on, but contributing little in receiving the body's weight when walking, passing that weight through an articulated action to the front of the foot and then adding strength to the taking of the next step. You can easily overlook the expressive potential of feet, ankles and legs. Feet, and their ability to balance and align the body, can play a huge role in the depiction of status, age, style and character.

The great ally of balance and control is gravity. Sadly, more of us seem to be at war with gravity, sagging under its influence or fighting against it with unnecessary tension, rather than learning to move in harmony with it. There is a point of equilibrium between yielding to gravity and resisting it. Man is a terrestrial creature. His prime element is the earth and when he has possession of the ground he can deal with the air, that element through which he communicates. In a state of equilibrium it is possible to feel the upward lift of the skeleton along the vertical centre line, and simultaneously, the downward relaxing of the muscles, as if they are hanging from the frame of the bones but ready and available for the next move.

To understand what I am describing requires considerable kinaesthetic sensitivity. There is a way of finding full height that uses so little muscular effort that it is almost impossible to feel which muscle group is actually doing the work. The spine can feel as though it is holding itself up and the head, which, for its volume, is the heaviest part of the body, is floating lightly beyond it. Go past that height and you should feel a limiting and tensing muscularity which is undesirable. The hard part is maintaining that lengthened spine and the floating head while allowing the muscle weight to flow down with the pull of gravity.

You can see the principle of opposition at work when you walk or run as you swing forward the opposite arm to the leading leg. To avoid lifting the shoulder and the whole side of the body as you raise an arm, you need to oppose the gesture by holding down the shoulder blade; to avoid the collapse of the torso as you bend your knees, you need to oppose the downward move with an upward energy release. To rise in a *relevée*, without loss of line and balance, you need to oppose the rising of the heels with the downward pressure of gravity through the shoulder line. We achieve control and line as the heels return to earth after a *relevée*, by opposing that lowering with the feeling in the upper body that makes it so pleasant to be up there you may never want to come down.

Another element in considering balance is weight change. The basic act of walking involves multiple changes of weight from foot to foot. Achieving a locomotion that is economical in its energy output, proficient in its coordination and characterised by a flow of body weight in whatever direction our intentions command is a skill to master. Most walks are flawed by incomplete weight changes. For general purposes, it is enough to share our weight somewhere between the two feet and therefore come to depend on both feet as we develop our signature walk. But theatre thrives on departures from the ordinary. If you neither stand nor walk well, it is little wonder that the extravagant and the non-naturalistic movement forms present problems. The neutral walk is a bridge that can link the natural and the stylised ways of moving and so make easier the transition from style to style and form to form.

The main barrier to acquiring new movement techniques is not always the material we are working with. More often than not, it is ourselves. For instance, walk very slowly and consciously complete a weight change with each step, and it becomes obvious how the upper and lower halves of the body rarely remain in alignment. Then make it more difficult by taking the steps in a series of different directions and lift the free leg off the floor to test the completion of the weight change. Then experience the upper half struggle to find its place over the base of the supporting leg.

The part of the body that every one of us allows to sag most easily seems to be the waist area, that boneless (except for the spine) section between the framework of the ribs and the bony girdle of the pelvis. That weakness in so central a position in the torso can't help but cause problems because it allows the upper body to drift out of alignment. Learning to align the whole body as a unity of parts on the vertical line, and to complete the full transfer of weight in a pattern of steps in random directions, with accompanying tilts, twists and displacements is a big part of the basics of studying Movement. That, and training the foot to be a secure foundation, reveals why walking is a reliable basis for formal movement techniques like dance and sports.

Most of the references to balance so far have concentrated on the idea of physical steadiness, but an example of being poised in a different state of balance could be the point of equilibrium between your own inner space and the outer physical environment in which you find yourself. Imbalance between these two spaces can easily rob you of calm and ease. If it's drama you want, then you'll find it when opposing forces operate on us to bring us out of balance both physically and emotionally. Any particular day of our social and professional lives will supply us with moments when we achieve, and when we lose that delicate set of balances.

3. Strength, stamina and aerobic fitness

Performing artists are their own equipment, kit of tools, library of memories and experiences, imaginings and instincts. They feed on their own energy. The concentration required during rehearsals and performances is intense and relentless. The mental, emotional and psychological controls are as demanding as the physical stamina required.

There is a special kind of strength and endurance in which nervous energy plays a great role, even if the part being enacted is a relatively static one. It differs from the muscularity and brute strength of an athlete for whom there is no necessity to conceal the effort involved. It is an inner strength of thought and emotion, intellect and aesthetics as much as of the body. You need to be in peak condition. Your work demands that of you, regardless of mood, health or misfortune. Whether a role is a major or minor one, whether the action is violent and exhausting or static and refined, your energy and stamina need to be greater than that of anything you will be called on to play.

Only when you are really fit will you find pleasure in engaging in energetic action, and only then is it possible to create new energy by using energy. Moreover, it is typical of theatre pieces that the action intensifies and the emotional stakes are highest as the performance builds to its conclusion, making it essential that the performer has reserves of stamina to do justice to the climactic moments. Hence the value of a regular personal-fitness regime for performers.

Such a program need not be dull or take up hours of the day. One of the best exercises is to stand and sit a little better than one ordinarily would, walk a bit quicker than usual, attack stairs two steps at a time, find excuses to run instead of walk. Many of the most common daily occupations can be converted into exercise if you lack the discipline of setting aside fixed periods for formal exercises. Picking up things from the floor provides a range of different stretches and crouches; towelling yourself in the bathroom offers a variety of bends, sways and isometric actions. Unless you set out purposefully to add bulk to a frail physique, I would advise you to find a program that has a strong aerobic element, and is based more on a process of lengthening the muscle fibres than contracting and bulking them. The strength that comes from length serves an actor best, allowing an outward flow of energy, a quicker response to impulse and the production of a neutral state. Better still, it avoids the bound quality and that fixed look that pumped-up muscularity produces.

'Let's work on getting some strength in that chest and in those arms. Shoulders, chest and extend to the finger tips!' Those words from Keith sound in my ears every time I get on the floor of a rehearsal room. He taught me to always start from a place of physical strength and clarity. Whether playing a dog, a nine-year-year old boy, or a normal man, I'm always reminded of the strength that Keith saw in that 19-year-old, 57kg weed.

MATTHEW WHITTET

4. Coordination and isolation control

I group these two together, even though the first quality suggests the unity of the body in action, and the second is about separateness. I see them as being the opposite ends of a single-line graph that need

EXERCISE IN COORDINATION

An exercise based on eurhythmics that might offer some assistance to improving coordination:

Start in a standing position and with the right arm outstretched and down by your side, do a three-count phrase (counting out the beats):

1. with the arm fully outstretched move it up in front of the body to arrive parallel to the ground (palm facing down).
2. the arm continues forward and upward in an arc to arrive vertical above your head (palm facing in).
3. the arm moves downward in an arc over the side of your body to arrive beside your body, fingers pointing towards the ground. Do this a number of times to allow the body to feel the phrase. Repeat with left arm.

Then practise a four-count phrase (again counting out the beats) starting with the right arm outstretched and down by your side:

1. with the arm fully outstretched move it up in front of the body to arrive parallel to the ground at shoulder height (palm facing down).
2. the arm continues forward in an arc to arrive vertical above your head (palm facing in).
3. the arm moves in an arc over the side of your body to arrive parallel to the ground at shoulder height (palm facing down).
4. the arm continues downward in the arc over the side of your body to arrive beside your body, hand pointing towards the ground. Do this a number of times to allow the body to feel the phrase. Repeat with left arm.

Now to a series of claps/beats do the three-count sequence with your right arm, at the same time doing the four-count sequence with your left arm, repeating until both arms finish down by your side again. Repeat with your right arm doing the four-count sequence, the left doing the three-count one.

When you have mastered this, take the sequence for a walk, first in a straight line, then challenge yourself by making random changes of direction.

MICHAEL CAMPBELL

each other to function. Coordination is the harmonious action that results from focusing all the body parts on a particular activity. In a well-coordinated person, a sort of body logic sees to it that the body finds the simplest and most economical way of undertaking an action whether or not that action is a new or a familiar one. There is an innate, congenital aspect to coordination. From babyhood it is evident that we are not all endowed with a comparable capacity.

A poorly coordinated actor can be a time-bomb when let loose in a constricted stage space, surrounded by props waiting to be dislodged, furniture asking to be bumped into, floor rugs crying out to be tripped over. To play a gauche character successfully, an actor needs coordinating skills of the highest order so that they can control their trips and bumps, create accidents and manage the ensuing havoc. The great French comedian Jacques Tati is a perfect example of this kind of actor.

Coordination is the big issue in compound and complex movement patterns where several body parts are involved at once. As in a dance sequence where the legs are busy with one set of rhythms and patterns and the arms, torso and head with others; or where you are involved in two or more distinct activities, like singing and walking, or continuing a complicated work function while involved in a discussion.

Complex moves are seldom merely physical feats. It is possible to improve in this vital area by breaking down the formidable concept of coordination into bits and working on the important contributing factors.

5. Peripheral vision

You will have little hope of control over space, and the details of what lies within it, if you can't see what's there. The reason certain actors take so little advantage of sets and props, the positioning and reactions of their cast members and especially the distances between them, must be that they don't notice them. Choices are always limited to what you are aware of. Nerves and intense concentration have the effect of allowing you to see only what you are looking at directly. It is impossible for you to take artistic advantage of all the perpetually changing circumstances that are being offered to you, unless you use both direct focus and peripheral vision.

6. Relaxation

Control of tension, economy of effort

To hear most people talk you would think that tension is just an inevitable part of living. It's difficult not to carry the tensions arising from one stressful situation into another. And the way to deal with the headaches, shoulder and neck pains and all the other restricting symptoms it produces, is to take a pill and ring the masseur for another appointment. Tension is not just physical, it is a composite of mental, muscular and emotional strain.

Let's face it, I'm never going to be Nureyev but the gift that Keith offered me has served me well. From less than perfect clay he left me with a permanent legacy and modicum of poise, lyricism and economy of movement.

MEL GIBSON

But surely, its opposite, relaxation— at least in the sense of complete and total physical relaxation—would render us even more inefficient. True relaxation would make us collapse and be useless. Some degree of tension is essential in everything we do. Obviously then, the intention should be to reduce effort to a minimum, and find the ideal balance between a tense and a relaxed condition.

EXERCISE IN RELAXATION

I find it works well to take the relaxing process through a series of stages. Begin lying on your back, eyes closed, arms heavy on the floor near your sides, legs in line with the torso and comfortably turned out. Then imagine images that encourage a state of general relaxation, such as imagining the floor under you is made of something that gives a pleasurable sensation—warm sand, a thick lamb's wool rug or black satin sheets—anything that would tempt you to release your spine and the whole surface of your back as if you wanted to melt into that surface.

Next, sense the weight of air above you and yield to the pressure of gravity. Open up the entire upper surface of your body to the light, and allow the warmth of the sun to enter and spread through you, again with that melting feeling. Then, assume the breath rhythm of deep sleep, where the exhalation period lasts seconds longer than the inward breath. And finally feel yourself sink a little deeper into the floor, exhaling and staying empty of air till the body demands a fresh intake.

In that same position, give yourself the time to locate, become aware of and release, the tension from each separate region of the body. Starting at the head, take your concentration downwards to the feet. The first port of call is the scalp, which you may find difficult to isolate and free of tightness, but which can bring great relief when it is eventually brought under control. Slowly travel down over the forehead and the eyebrows, around the eyes, over the cheeks, around the mouth and the jaw line. Some of the more notorious centres of tension—the neck, shoulders, ribcage and elbows—may need extra time, repetition and attention.

A variation on this procedure leading to deeper states of relaxation is to increase the tension in a body part such as the face or a leg or an arm. Hold that tension for a few seconds and then let go. Repeat, sometimes in a sudden release, sometimes very gradually, till the opposite condition is reached.

Another stage in the process of recognising our own patterns of tension could be to ask someone to manipulate you in a gentle series of lifts and movements of the hands, arms, shoulders, legs and head. You should not attempt to resist or assist the sequence in any way. This exercise has the added advantage of allowing the operator to learn about their own body at the same time as manipulating yours.

The difficulty of isolating certain muscle groups, and the stubbornness of others to unlock and relax, can come as a surprise. But the experience of complete relaxation is a helpful first step in the task of achieving economy of effort in movement. You need awareness of, and control over, both tension and relaxation if you are to achieve that point of ideal balance. Remember, too, that degrees of both these qualities will be distinguishing marks of all characterisations, and must be considered as essential aspects of the inner-outer life of the roles you will play. It is too common to see actors using tension as a substitute for emotion, forcing and squeezing out the emotional states they manufacture in their attempt at dramatic realisations.

On Our Selection: l to r Don Crosby, John Clayton, Geoffrey Rush, Kerry Walker, Mel Gibson, Sally Cahill. Dir George Whaley, Chor. Keith Bain, Jane Street Theatre 1979.

7. Flexibility

Agility, stillness

Audiences love the virtuosity of flexible movers, choreographers enjoy the challenge of exploiting the capabilities of loose, supple bodies. And who can blame the tight and inflexible ones for longing to know what it feels like to exchange pain and strain for the ease of splits, high kicks and deep bends that others enjoy? But it is often overlooked that even in dance and gymnastics, flexibility needs to be nurtured with a corresponding strengthening process for the sake of control and safety. Unless care is taken to provide a well-graded exercise program to achieve suppleness, terrible damage can be done. Of course it is an advantage for an actor to have the versatility that suppleness and body fluency can give, but for general purposes it is no big deal if this is not the case. It is a rare role that demands extraordinary looseness.

Agility is concerned less with extremes of body mobility and more with alertness and a facility for sudden and nimble action. It is charac-terised by a readiness to move off in any direction, to be able to dodge and weave and to manipulate a space and all that it contains with confidence, judgment and accuracy. I have known actors sadly lacking in such skills whose careers have never presented them with the need to demonstrate this sort of gymnastic ability. Equally, I have helped train others who have built their reputations largely on daring and physical prowess. My favourite actors are the versatile ones as capable of softness as they are of strength, of sensitivity and restraint, as they are of explosive energy and menace, and who are blessed with the gift of balancing the male/female, the serious/funny, the intellectual/physical, the lyrical/coarse and the sophisticated/common dichotomies present in human nature.

At the opposite end of the agility spectrum sits the rare and difficult ability to be still. Everything about our structure and inner make-up seems so designed for movement that stillness, for many people, is the hardest thing we could ever ask them to achieve. Stillness, or at least a state of much reduced activity, can carry astonishing force. It can intensify the impact and pressure of what is being said, felt and thought, and release these with a directness of projection that is often not present when there is movement to accompany them.

It is desirable to maintain a balance between exercising and conditioning the large muscle groups and understanding the significance of little movements and the subtleties of the small muscle groups. Hands, fingers, feet, wrists and faces need as much care and exercise as spines, legs and arms. The tiny muscles just under the skin, around the eyes and mouth, between the ribs and over the torso can be easily neglected, even though awareness and control of these is essential for the actors' range and subtlety of expression. It is useful for you to check the comparative time you give to big muscle group stretching and strengthening, and that given to the fine detailing of small muscle control of the gestures of the head, neck, shoulders and ribs.

Our Western theatre traditions have led us to value production styles that push the action along at all costs, that emphasise contrast and changes of pace, as if contemporary audiences are incapable of enduring slow movement and stillness. I would go so far as to say that a lot of the movement in Western theatre productions adds little to the performance, and is there to help the actors get through the piece rather than to enrich its meaning for the audience. One thing about stillness is certain: it is an extended moment of inner and outer life and must be rich in content to be of artistic and expressive value. It is most dramatic when the thought and the intention are not quite complete, so that the stillness expresses the drama of the unfinished moment and the expectation of what is yet to happen. A still exterior needs the fullness and pressure of inner life, continuously transmitted, to have optimum dramatic impact. An empty stillness is a deadly vacuum.

I have never found anybody who could make stillness so interesting, or walking so interesting, as Keith, or make basic gestures so detailed, and show how the way you look at somebody is so much about how you feel about them. It was the truth and honesty in the movement that Keith was always so particular about.

JANE MISKOVIC

From a technical viewpoint, stillness is best achieved by control from one's deepest centre. It is hardest to maintain when that sense of centre is less strong than the peripherals of the body. While a few fortunate souls possess a natural composure and physical calm, many more of us exhibit a fidgety restlessness characterised by constant weight changes, unnecessary gestures like scratching and rubbing, rocking, twitching and fiddling, seemingly prompted by over-production of percussive or nervous energy. For such people stillness is a problem to achieve and an agony to maintain.

Qualities that enrich the kinaesthetic response

These qualities help you to know and feel, rather than just do:

1. Body awareness, body memory;
2. Body image, body confidence, physical courage, the breaking of inhibitions, emotional coverage and success, presence, pride, respect and acceptance of self;
3. Recognition and control of mannerisms;
4. Centring.

1. Body awareness, body memory

Awareness allows you to distinguish between one state of being and feeling and another. Awareness is essential for the development of body memory, empathetic and accurate learning, spatial definition and a sense of space and time. Through it you will come to recognise your personal mannerisms, inhibitions and recurring habits of response. It is awareness that grants you objectivity towards that most subjective entity, you. Without it you are flying blind.

On the other hand, you depend on your five senses of sight, hearing, smell, touch and taste to accurately inform you about the world. It is an aspect of Movement training to sharpen these senses to their greatest degree and so allow you the richest possible response to whatever environment you inhabit, including the performing space. The more richly your senses absorb the atmospheres and details of your surroundings, the greater the treasury of sensory memories and references you have to recall. The more observant and appreciative you become of all that these senses reveal, the more your imagination will be fed and your choices increased.

But these five senses don't build your knowledge of yourself to anything like the same degree that they tell us about everything and everybody. You will never see yourself as others do. You will never see your own performances. Even films, photographs and videos fail to give the whole picture, because the subjectivity attached to viewing yourself stands in the way of knowing how you are received and perceived by others. I can safely say that we are all constantly surprised and disturbed by the manner in which we are perceived, compared with the impression we felt sure we were making.

You can't change or modify what you are not aware of. Doors that would give access to the skills and techniques every versatile performer would love to possess will remain closed to anyone lacking this gift of self-awareness. I strongly recommend the writings of Moshe Feldenkrais especially *Awareness Through Movement*.*

2. Body image

This list embraces qualities that are as much a matter of attitude as they are of physicality and technical prowess: body confidence, physical courage; the breaking of inhibitions; emotional courage and access; presence; pride; respect and acceptance of self, openness to impulse.

They are about how you see yourself, how you value yourself and how you balance your positive and negative feelings about yourself and your working relationships. They are fragile qualities, more easily crushed

---

*   Moshe Feldenkrais (1904–84) was an Israeli physicist and the founder of the Feldenkrais Method, designed to reduce pain and improve human functioning by increasing self-awareness through movement.

than strengthened, but fundamental to success. These are attitudes and attributes that are difficult to acquire without the many forms of help which good teaching can supply.

If you go through the list slowly and consider the positive implications of each item, separately at first and then as a whole, I hope you will recognise them as individually valuable and collectively essential. Think of them negatively: 'What if I lacked each or all of these?' and it should be evident that success as an actor would be a near impossibility. Let us take them one by one:

Body confidence

To lack self-confidence is like having someone—yourself—getting totally in your way. Its effect is to make you the focus of your concern, and not the matter in hand. It inhibits your movement, weakens the impact of personality, restricts the natural voice, kills off spontaneity and spreads unease among your audience. We have all felt it and know it to be a devastating sensation.

Your body needs victories and successes for confidence to grow. No one develops a belief in their own abilities if the set tasks are offered in such a way that difficulty and failure are more likely to be the outcome than comprehension and success. To conquer challenges, and so build confidence, work on your ability to break down material into digestible portions.

All of us face situations that shake our confidence and test our ability to perform well. Even though we might be shaking inside, with our head and heart in a mad flutter, it is possible to present an appearance of self-possession that will convince others of your calm confidence, and do wonders for your own powers of centeredness and control.

I realised that the whole element of Movement work was going to be a challenge. But Keith was a gentle leader and certainly wasn't about to dismantle people's egos. He carefully, diligently and, more often than not, hilariously, led the actors in our class to an understanding of their bodies that they would never have imagined.
RICHARD ROXBURGH

EXERCISE FOR CONFIDENCE
Run, Freeze, Turn, Walk, Balance, Fall back, Run
It would start by the students repeating this list of actions in order. After the first round Keith would suggest they could be more daring, that perhaps one of their walks could be a 'silly' walk or their balances more challenging, or their turns more spectacular. Gradually as the possibilities opened up and the students became more confident Keith would encourage interaction and after several repetitions they would be lifting each other, moving in and around other people with great freedom and playfulness. By repeating this exercise over and over the students not only became bolder and more daring but also more sensitive and aware.

ANCA FRANKENHAEUSER

Physical courage, the breaking of inhibitions, emotional courage and access

It doesn't always follow that someone who is coordinated and strong is also physically brave. Athletic and competent movers can be terrified of heights, nervous of being lifted or caught or carried, and disconcerted whenever out of an upright stance. The thrill that some people find in tumbling, falling, cartwheeling can be sheer terror for others. I have seen otherwise confident actors go pale at the thought that I might ask them to climb a ladder, swing by a rope or move along a narrow catwalk, step on and off a moving revolve, let alone hang upside down or fall from a platform, no matter what safety precautions have been set in place.

Usually, at the very first rehearsal of a new show, the designer begins by showing a model of the set to the cast, who all go 'ooh' and 'aah' with excitement at the costumes and the design. And probably because the model itself is so small and neat they feel sure that steeply raked ramp, that staircase with no handrail, the suspended walkway and the trapdoor will all be a piece of cake when the time comes. Actors who recognise their lack of physical courage can help themselves overcome this to a degree by privately practising simple things like climbing a ladder, stepping up onto a chair, standing on a table and persisting with basic acrobatic rolls and tumbles. But beware, courage without technique could literally be death or disaster for any actor.

I'm reminded of being involved in many elaborate productions where the sets have been so complicated, costly and mechanically intricate that their special features and apparatus could not be reproduced in the rehearsal room. That meant walking into the usual bleak rehearsal space to find a bewildering pattern of taped markings covering the stage space and representing all the things you most needed but couldn't have—the steps and stairs, the revolves, the lifts, the rostra and suspended platforms.

The problems a director and choreographer might have to face in realising their concept might include having to imagine the difficulties associated with, say, setting movement for Jesus, Mary and the twelve apostles to sing and dance on a set for *Jesus Christ Superstar* that will eventually comprise design elements that open and shut, move up, down and around, tilt and suspend. They might have to calculate how long it would take for sixteen choristers dressed in crinolines or high-heeled shoes to enter down an imaginary sloping ramp, or a staircase steeper than any in real life; or decide what movement or dance effects could be safely asked of a cast of Penzantian pirates singing their way down from non-existent rigging. A prime worry is the effect on the performers of climbing and leaping about on a set that arrives complete only in time for final rehearsals. While an audience has little awareness of the courage demanded of an actor in those productions that provide their special thrills, actors themselves are often forced to be braver than they ever dreamed they could be.

The effect of fear and inhibition is to hold back what we most want to communicate—our thoughts, emotions and actions. That puts an end to any chance of being free of yourself. It makes you the problem and not the demands of the situation. Within a larger group, and with clear, objective freedom rather than instruction, it is possible, if only for one moment at a time, to be distracted from your self-absorption, soak up the group energy and catch the atmosphere of other people's confidence. Conversely, the one-by-one approach sometimes experienced in a class can throw all attention onto you, making you feel a victim of the instruction, the space, the tutor, the rest of the class and the system.

It is not always the big issues of Movement that are the greatest causes of inhibiting distress. Touching another person, being touched by someone else, being embraced or manhandled, receiving or transmitting a direct look, sweating, lying or rolling on the floor, being alone in a big space, falling, running, balancing are just a few of the dreads from which some of us suffer and which require patience and help to overcome. Points of technique that the majority love to play with may be the last things that we want to face—such as exercises for flexibility, rhythm, coordination, space sense and body memory. Since the lack of these qualities has been a long-standing cause of embarrassment and frustration, it is no surprise that many of us develop phobias and scars on their account.

It's rare to find people totally open, unprejudiced, unjudgmental and unfearful of every Movement form and skill that an actor's training includes. You may be accepting of a great many, but are certain to be intimidated by, terrified of, or feel superior towards many more.

Presence

This attribute may be difficult to define in words but we recognise its unmistakable quality when we meet it in another person. It begins with good alignment, releasing into the space around you qualities of your personality, authority and assurance. It registers as an aura that attracts our notice, a personal atmosphere that can be felt as well as seen, an air that radiates from within to surprising distances beyond the body's limits. It's a charismatic state that proclaims status, creates focus and demands attention.

A person's presence need not be a warm one. It may chill the air, intimidate or create an unsettling tension. Writers describe their characters' presence in such terms as powerful, timid, overbearing, sexy, menacing—not all admirable terms by any means. We can all name cult and gang leaders, religious and political figures whose potent presence accounts for the appalling power they exert over their followers. And others whose magnetic personality radiates magnanimity.

It is probably easier to list some of the effects that hinder the creation of such presence; for example fidgeting, squirming, indefinite and indirect gesturing and focus. But when the inner life is fully animated, an interested and curious concentration is present, high energy levels and confident self-esteem abound, it doesn't matter much what's happening on the outside so long as the inner lights are shining strongly. Many of the topics I have discussed elsewhere in this book have relevance to this matter of presence: alignment, the capacity to transmit and to receive; and the ability to balance our inner space with the outer spaces in which we function. There is little chance of maintaining a presence that charms and inspires if we feel victimised or disconcerted by the conditions and occasions we face. A state of strong centeredness, economy of effort, a variety of open windows or release points in our body, control and an even temperament are other vital ingredients. When an actor possesses a powerful presence, representing vulnerability can be difficult; but the lack of personal presence, or the incapacity to portray it, leaves a huge gap in the armoury of any actor.

Finally, the essential thing about presence is being *present*, with such personal force that the mere potential for action is as promising as any real action that might take place. In the early stages of your training, the search for how to build a powerful presence can be one of the biggest challenges.

Pride, respect and acceptance of self, a healthy self-image

As the body is your instrument, you must develop an acceptance of its attributes and its shortcomings. You must look at yourself objectively: the more physically aware you become the greater your capacity to be an expressive actor. It is through exploration, through actively experiencing and engaging in physical activity, that you can begin to discover your body's strengths and limitations. By extending your range and physical ability you begin to recognise and acknowledge your body's potential. Take every opportunity to be open and brave, to free your inhibitions and self-doubt, to develop physical confidence and pride in your work. It is also important that you allow yourself to be carefully guided so that you can develop a healthy respect for the dangers inherent in robust physical activity—you must learn to trust yourself and those who are working with you so that you, and they, can be daring and still feel secure. Developing these attributes should be a key focus of the early stages of your movement training.

An openness to impulse

Having gained a degree of physical confidence and awareness, you should then be capable of being open to impulse in a variety of circumstances. The mind and body work together so that the body responds freely to the impulses that arise from thoughts and emotions. When you can trust your body and not be inhibited or embarrassed, you can simply respond. This freedom can lead to discoveries and insights that can inform your work, and by remaining open to impulse you are also inviting the audience to engage with you. It is equally important to remain open to other actors, to be able to react and respond to impulses as they arise. By maintaining this openness to impulse you remain alive, present and in the moment.

3. Recognition and control of mannerisms

Mannerisms are those peculiarities of behaviour and speech that we are often guilty of using excessively, without being conscious of how ingrained they are. They are our physical signature tunes that arise from our energy levels, our temperament and the influences of our upbringing. They help us feel at home in our body. We learn to depend on them to support our self-image. They can be ways of concealing what we don't want others to see, or of coping with insecurity and tricky circumstances. They can also betray us with give-away evidence of our real self. They are the basis for much of the image others have of us.

If untended they also can set limits to our expressiveness. We can overwork our most favoured mannerisms by using them indiscriminately. Some are quite endearing. You can see this in others: you can love someone's way of tilting the head, their way of tucking their hair behind their ear, the flicking energy of their hand gestures, their constant changing of weight or a habit of biting their lip. Other mannerisms are distracting and irritating, as when someone is perpetually fidgeting or fiddling. Some add to the clarity and truth of their body statements while others are affectations or distractions from the revelation of their real self.

It is pretty inevitable that if you, as an actor, are unaware of your own recurring habits you will take a goodly selection on stage with you. Till you recognise your own habits by catching yourself in action in a variety of activities, or have them revealed to you by teachers and friends, you are never likely to know which ones will be of service to your craft and which you should leave in the dressing-room. There are still shocks to be had, despite your best attempts at self-perception, when you see yourself on film or hear what you sound like on a recording. Even the occasional glimpse of your reflection in a mirror can come as a surprise, and not always a pleasant one.

The dangers come when you ask a limited range of gestures and movement to be the means of expressing precise states of feeling in a variety of characters and circumstances. Until your self-analysis is accurate and discerning, you will continue to ask your audience to watch a regurgitation of your own persistent behaviour. Acting is so much a matter of who you are not. The lives you are exploring as an actor are lives you have never lived. Your own reactions and dynamics are not likely to serve the experiences and specific nature of most of the roles you will play. I attribute the attrition rate of actors in the profession, many of whom start spectacularly but fade away after a few years, to the sameness of their characterisations and the mannerisms of their voice and body. This is as much a failure to get to know themselves, as a failure to enter into the nature of their characters.

Fortunately, actors exist who enchant by achieving a depth of empathy and identification with a role that allows them to surrender themselves to that vision and re-emerge in the persona of another. But this careful editing of performance to eliminate what is unnecessary or inappropriate, and to refine only those aspects of physicality that truly reveal the role, is not always the strongest point of an actor's method of preparation. There are fine and popular actors who are treasured for playing very close to themselves and who are encouraged to bring their special brand of personality, charisma or idiosyncrasies to each of their appearances. But we're talking about special talents here, including some great comedians, villains and heroes. In their case it is their outstandingly individual and distinctive manner that is the source of their success.

4. Centring

Nowhere is a subject more confusing, abstruse, full of philosophic overtones, physiological detail and transcendental implications than centring. The word 'centre' has been made to mean so many things that it is hard to define it. If I were given the instruction, 'Get in touch with your centre', I would not know where to begin. Is there an exact spot where my essence is concentrated? Do I have only one C-spot from which might emanate the energies powering my movement and the emotions that warm, chill, expand and contract my super-sensitive body? Does it mean my centre of gravity? Or my centre of weight, which I can adjust at will and which fluctuates with my moods, my physical and emotional well-being and my age? Or is it, perhaps, that core of inner focus that I manage to contact on the odd occasions when I have succeeded in bringing the full force of my thinking and feeling to the services of the task in hand? Does it refer to that line of vertical strength that supports me in my balance, gives me central support when I spin and turn, and which, when released beyond me through the crown of my head as if it were my extended aerial, gives me a claim to the space above me and adds power to my presence? I can accept centre as meaning all these things. The more wide-ranging the definition is, the more ways it is possible to apply the concept to practical purpose.

I find the notion of a dynamic centre to be a very helpful one for the same reasons that I have mentioned before of building self-perception, defining a character and creating a centrally based physicalisation and transformation. No matter how exactly people describe the location of an ideal body centre, it is plain to see how many of us are exceptions to any such rule. Watch any group of passers by: their walk and actions will be distinguished as much by where in the body their engine is located, the dynamo that sets them into action, as by any other differentiating feature.

Some centres are easy to discern. For instance, in many of us the head appears to lead and the rest of the body obediently follows. In this case—which can be a stereotypical way of representing a snooping, suspicious busybody of a character—the head is generally forward of the body's vertical line. The shoulders can be another dynamic centre for movement. Here, new movement is initiated by a lurching action of the shoulder line and often continues with the shoulders swinging in opposition to the legs in the stereotype of a cowboy. The chest becomes

The Cobra: Mark Lee and Robert Helpmann. Dir. Richard Wherrett, Chor. Keith Bain, Sydney Theatre Company 1983.

the dynamic centre for some, the stomach, in the case of pregnant women and corpulent men, as do the hips, the pelvis, the arms and the legs for others. I have seen some very subtle forms of dynamic centring. For instance, there are those who seem pulled forward by upper body parts, and others apparently pushed forward from the buttocks, the pelvis and the small of the back. Even more subtle flavours become obvious when fists, fingers, wrists, elbows, foreheads, noses, chins, feet, knees and thighs, play prominent roles in activating and colouring an individual's movement.

Similarly, there are those whom I call hand, eye, eyebrow, mouth, throat people; others I call leg walkers because their legs walk off carrying the upper body with them like a passenger, as though all the decision-making and energy creation is done in the lower limbs. Foot people can vary from those whose feet hang like dead things from the end of their legs, contributing nothing to either take-off or landing, through degrees of turn-in and turn-out, to what my father used to call a spring-heeled Jack, whose powerful press up from the arch lifted the heel, and in turn the whole body, giving him a loping kind of locomotion.

If you experiment with these habitual expressions of centredness, using sensitivity, empathy and imagination, they can become a useful means of entering the sensibilities of the other characters, of sampling their self-image and seeing the world through their eyes and feelings. That is what should be the aim of any such experiment—certainly not to develop a superficial facility to reproduce funny walks and oddities of mannerism, but to get closer to the inner states of others in the difficult process of identification and transformation.

Experimenting with the variations are endless: walking wider, then narrower than you normally do; more turned out, less turned out; taking longer strides, taking shorter steps; leading from a variety of dynamic centres; maintaining a vertical postural line, then taking the body in a more forward alignment, angling the body line backward; using the full length of the leg, or never quite straightening either knee; increasing the rise and fall in a walk, removing any such lilt; lengthening the body to achieve a sense of corporeal unity, relaxing to a point where the body registers as a collection of separate parts.

There is probably no better example of how huge a change of inner life can result from a minimal outer adjustment than trying the following arm movements. First rotate slightly the arm in the shoulder joint to allow the back of the hand to lead in an arm swing. Let your whole inner life and your perceptions be affected by this. Then try regulating the arm position so that the thumb edge of the hand is directed forward in the swing. After letting the effect of that soak in, rotate the arm till the inside of the wrist is presented to the front, and compare the values and the self-perceptions that have occurred. When you reach the stage of being able to justify, psychologically, any of these tiny adjustments to your own physicalisation, the distances from yourself you are capable of travelling, and the conviction established as the inner and outer forces connect in a single power, it will be something to be marvelled at.

Technical Qualities

Audiences are quick to give meaning to all the technical things that an actor does. This is the same in real life where details of physicality become symbols of inner qualities. For instance, we tend to give someone who is outwardly alert, direct and confident the benefit of possessing these same qualities of temperament and intellect. Conversely, a de-energised look, a wandering focus, slow body rhythms and sloppy carriage are frequently taken to be evidence of mental and personal carelessness.

Technical qualities arise from an understanding of the elements and the theories of Movement and acting. Specifically an actor needs:

1. A space sense and an appreciation of all the implications for an actor that arise from the concept of space;
2. A sense of time, of timing, and of rhythm, and an appreciation of all that the concept of time holds for an actor;

3. A wide dynamic range and, again, an understanding of the concepts of weight, energy and dynamics as they apply to actor training.

These qualities—of Space, Time, Energy/Weight/Dynamics— are so intrinsic to the technical study of Movement, that a separate chapter has been devoted to them.

4. The ability to connect the strands of an integrated course of training— acting, movement and voice—and to transfer the explorations and discoveries of the classroom into professional practice.

It is very important for you to be able to apply your technical training to scene work and performance. Movement classes often will allow you to explore aspects of your character's physicality which you can then take into rehearsals. Warm-ups can also help develop the ability to connect different aspects of your technique and training to achieve a quality performance.

5. The capacity to improvise on given themes with surrender and courage.

It is also important that you are able to apply your imagination as well as your technical skills to your preparation for performance. By exploring freely and openly in class, rehearsal and improvisations, discoveries can be made that are more organic than intellectual. Appreciate the insights gained through surrendering in improvisations and value them as highly as those arrived at by analysis and research. By responding to impulse, by allowing the body to react and trusting the body 'brain', a more detailed and believable character will emerge.

6. Judgment and taste in details and choices; a sense of style; obser-vational analysis.

In applying observational skills, you need to look closely at the people who surround you with curiosity, openness and empathy. In that way you can learn to appreciate the myriad of details that can enlighten and inform your work. By closely observing humanity in all its guises you will pick up on things beyond the corporeal—the things that make each of us unique. By deep observation it is hoped that you would also acquire a sense of style and judgement.

By watching fellow actors in rehearsal, you will learn judgement in making choices for your own work.

The basic skills you learn change from year to year. When I was at NIDA people still did things like fencing and ballet. We did social dances of all types. Probably more important than learning those particular dances or movement tasks was the job of having to learn them. Sometimes professionalism is just how quickly you can pick something up.

RUPERT BURNS

7. A strong compositional component to extend the actor's creative processes:

As you become more confident in your ability to be open, responsive and physically engaged in your work you may begin to recognise that you are capable of creating original work. Movement classes can incorporate opportunities for the students to workshop, devise and create their own material. In this environment you could be encouraged to work cooperatively and collaboratively, to share ideas and explore possibilities. Given set guidelines, you may be able to create anything from short sequences to site-specific performances and full theatrical productions. By watching and appreciating other's work, you can develop confidence in your own ideas and their ability to translate them into action.

Compositional understanding will also enhance your ability to appreciate the structure, form and style of each production you prepare for. It will allow you to contribute ideas and concepts confidently and to engage more fully in the creative process.

A selection of techniques

The following techniques are associated with the skills areas appropriate for an actor's work.

1. Bows, curtsies, protocol for period and costume plays, fans, fashion styles;
2. Handling props;
3. Martial arts, stage fights, armed and unarmed combat, fencing;
4. Yoga;
5. Circus skills, including clowning, juggling, skating, aerial and stilt work; vaudevillian routines;
6. Historical, folk, social, national, character dance, jazz, tap, ballet, butoh;
7. Mime and mask work, commedia dell' arte;
8. Acrobatics, falls, release work and partnering;
9. Military drill.

Of these only the first two need discussion here as the others are techniques with well established and documented methods for the skills appropriate to each discipline.

Barn Dance, *On Our Selection:* Dir. George Whaley, Chor. Keith Bain, Jane Street Theatre 1979.

1. Bows, curtsies, protocol for period and costume plays, fans, fashion styles

I have spent years watching Australian actors find what should be a joy of styled and period movement become an uneasy, self-conscious experience. Their attempts to assume an appropriate bearing robs them of the truth of the role. And yet I have also seen the ease and relish with which the same actors slide down the social ladder—spit, scratch, slouch and lurch without the least loss of composure or conviction. It is not necessarily inhibition or lack of imagination that robs the actor

Miranda Otto in *The Caucasian Chalk Circle:* Dir. John Clark, NIDA/Sydney Theatre Company 1989.

EXERCISE

Preparation for the basse dance

Before teaching the processional court dance, *The Basse Dance*, which was danced before and through the Medieval period and into the Renaissance, Keith would, while they were walking, take the students through what they would have been wearing, imagine how that might feel and, because of that, respond with an appropriate style of moving. First he would explain: 'It's about taking on the appropriate style for whatever you need to do and that you have to believe that you can be on another scale, *be* grand, and surrender to the *quality.*'

Keith's description of the clothes included:

WOMEN: a headdress or cone hat with silk fabric attached to the top and broad ribbon under the chin. Long dress with tight bodice, sleeves with wide opening and a long train/trail, requiring the wearer to bend their knees. Pick up the train in one hand and feel the weight of the fabric. Soft pointy shoes.

MEN: a hat like a beret with a plume, tights and a beautiful jacket, A belt holding a sword on your left side. Soft pointy shoes.

JULIA COTTON AND ANCA FRANKENHAUSER

of effectiveness when he is asked to leave behind his modern qualities and illuminate a period of society distinctly different from his own. It can simply be that he has been let down, even betrayed, by his body.

Many costumes and their accessories require adjustments to posture, to gesture, to space use and to the style of behaviour, which, when well-executed, add greatly to the truth of the piece. The casualness of modern apparel, and thus the slumps it encourages, give today's actors no practice in the subtleties of bodily adjustments that more formal fashion demands. A heeled shoe or a business suit can make life difficult for a young actor whose day-to-day wardrobe consists of T-shirts, torn jeans and runners. Not every modern actress responds easily to corsets, hoops, hats, high heels and long trains. In most plays the extraordinary nature of earlier fashion periods must be made to appear absolutely normal for the characters portrayed. Even without a range of outfits for class or room use, there are a thousand ways to help an actor understand the logic that underlies each period's fashion.

It makes a big difference to see an actor really use their costume, rather than being worn by it. Keith taught us how to find the restrictions of the costume, and in what way that could help form what you are doing physically and emotionally. I think I practically graduated in costume wearing when I went to NIDA. I had one with this huge headpiece and spectacular makeup and big sleeves and enormous skirt. And here on the belt was a bicycle cog. I remember going to ask Keith how to walk with a train: It's a momentum thing, turn quickly and the train will turn, but if you just droop around you will trip on the dress.

MIRANDA OTTO

2. Handling props

I have seen actors being made a fool of, or upstaged, by a bloody-minded prop to a greater extent than by a fellow actor. Most actors tell stories of the door that wouldn't open, the doorknob that came off in the hand, the match that won't light, the bottle or glass that falls and breaks, the button that won't undo, the fan that won't open. Not all of these incidents are the fault of the actor, but many are. Quite often the prop and its appropriate handling are crucial to the effectiveness of the scene and any clumsiness on the part of an actor can be detrimental to the truth of the character and destroy the rhythm and atmosphere of the performance.

Every single article, each piece of furniture, everything that an actor touches, plays with, puts to use, needs to be endowed with the specific qualities appropriate to the character and the circumstances. It

I hear him over my shoulder whenever I am rehearsing. One particular quote of his that I use always is, 'Nothing will undo a performance faster than a mishandled prop.' And it's so true!

GLENN HAZELDINE

must be transformed from a mere stage prop into a reality essential to the actor's performance. Just as an actor needs to transform his fellow cast members into the characters they must be to complete their own transformation, so they must transform the set and all its details. Every aspect of it must be explored to discover its relevance to the character and their history, its usefulness as an obstacle or an ally and, most of all, how the qualities of the role can be revealed by the way the props are perceived and handled.

You can experiment with these ideas using the simplest of materials. Tables, chairs, articles of clothing, books and bags, windows and doors, walls and curtains will serve for explorations of endowment, dramatic possibility, expertise or awkwardness, details of mood, temperament, social status and period. Taking time to understand the way in which a prop responds to your manipulation is valuable research. Revealing both competence and clumsiness requires coordination and skill. Clumsiness, in particular, requires superb coordination, great spatial judgment, clever use of peripheral vision and a sense of timing—all, of course, magnificently concealed.

Everything that an actor comes into contact with, or uses in any way during performance, is an aid to making clearer the details of the character's story. By the way you sit on a chair, for example, might tell the audience it is a familiar and loved possession in a congenial environment, or a stiff, uncomfortable, distasteful object in a shabby and unfamiliar one. These are details that would be infinitely more difficult to reveal without the chair.

Things don't even need to be touched. Merely looking at, dismissing with a glance or ignoring an object can convey strong feelings of love, envy or frustration that otherwise might require a whole scene to make apparent. A concern for detail and an appreciation of the ways character and motive are clarified by interaction with props and objects can be explored through imaginative experiments.

Personal and professional disciplines

These are disciplines that are appropriate to the career of a theatre artist.

- The double capacity to cooperate and collaborate with others as well as to maintain a personal method for working alone;
- Un-judgmental curiosity about the behaviour and the inner and outer lives of the human race; generosity of spirit; a preparedness to make oneself fully available to others and an appreciation for what is offered by one's fellow actors;
- A sensitivity to creating an environment necessary for brave creative work; self-discipline, concentration, punctuality, general courtesy.

If you want a flexible body and therefore a flexible mind, and the ability to play a variety of things, then you have to use your body and you have to keep this tool flexible. You need constant awareness, from your front to your back. Not only when you're working on stage, but when you're in front of the camera. You need to know where everyone and everything else is. And therefore how you physically fit into the picture you are all creating.

Keith encouraged people to understand space from a visceral, personal place and also to have an innate sense of ensemble. How to work with other actors. To have a sense of the whole, not just about the specifics. To have a sense of the picture you are collectively trying to create.

It's about having objectivity.

CATE BLANCHETT

5

The Blessed Trinity of Movement

Keith's teaching ranged from gentle reminders for men
in tights 'to pack their lunch boxes properly' to instilling
an awareness of the instinctive and emotional impulse to
movement. He taught us to claim the space we inhabited,
to feel good about who we were as physical beings.
I became acutely aware of the power of minute, economic
movement; of stillness and silence. He is a sort of guru.

HUGO WEAVING

Space, time and the combined power of weight/energy/dynamics is the
blessed trinity of Movement. Like all great truths and natural laws,
once they have been revealed they are self-evident and indisputable.

Humans are so naturally mobile that our movements are mostly
experienced and witnessed as units of activity. If I make an open-armed
gesture, turn my head and eyes from one point of focus to another and
take a step and a change of weight in any direction, what I would register
most clearly would be the starting position, the movements felt, and
finally the end position. However, in doing any one of this combination

Hugo Weaving as Duke of Brachiano in *The White Devil,* with Philip Quast. Dir. Gale Edwards, Movement Keith Bain, Sydney Theatre Company 2000.

of actions, I would have travelled through a million distinct points, moments of space, each with its own potential for meaning, design and dynamics. I could have paused at any one or any number of such points, played games with my energy use and my rhythms and timings, suspended and alternated the movement of the limbs. In short, I could have broken down the whole into thousands of tiny, telling moments.

Space

Space challenges us every moment of the day. It never ceases to offer us opportunities. In performance it needs to be tamed and exploited. In each of the spaces we occupy, there is an appropriate position, angle, range and shaping for our purpose. Space is one of our greatest allies and servants, and to work in harmony with it adds to our power and effectiveness. For some it is also a deadly enemy and a traitorous companion, able to reduce, embarrass and frustrate us, making us self-conscious and

Keith developed crucial spatial awareness, knowledge of stage space and its weak and strong areas, conscious use of balance and asymmetry, readable relationships between actors, angling the body, avoiding full frontals, creative groupings, as well as highly-developed peripheral vision, and (like a Noh actor) an ability to see oneself from the audience.

AUBREY MELLOR

ineffectual. Lacking a reasonably reliable sense of space makes you not only a menace to yourself but a danger to your fellow performers.

Space has its own divisions and categories. Most obviously, space is our environment, from our most intimate and personal space to every possible space you might enter, or imagine. You come to know certain spaces intimately, with pleasure or distaste; on the other hand, you confront new spaces practically every moment.

Much of this is imposed and you can only accept it and adapt. Much you can change, put to your own purposes. How you use space is a key to your individuality. How much space you need is another such key. How you read other people's use of space is the basis on which you interpret them and their relationship with you. You come to know yourself largely from how you feel about the range of spaces in which you find yourself, and the people and objects that occupy and share your space. It is through space that you make contact with everything and everybody you encounter. All your forms of communication are made through space and your response to it changes as you pass from infancy to old age.

Years ago, I attended a picnic in the shade of a spreading tree in a public park in the midday heat of a summer Sunday. The occasion was a farewell to a young couple and their two small sons. The gathering included newborn babes, crawling infants, children running and climbing, singles, couples, seniors and one old lady in her nineties. Each of us knew only a few of the entire group. Only the host couple knew everyone.

Ignoring the time and energy considerations, the spatial picture and its story was fascinating: from the first arrivals variously making their entrances across the lawns, past the trees and gardens to the appointed spot, to the patterns of meetings and greetings, groupings and regroupings indicating the differing degrees of familiarity among those present. The total design was a kaleidoscope of shifting bodies, rugs, shadows and sunlight, hampers, strollers, food platters and glassware and the trails of smoke from the barbecue. The individual body shapes, each telling the story of each person's age, mood, self-image, comfort or discomfort, degree of enjoyment, degree of intimacy, to the shaping and re-shaping of the whole group over the hours the picnic lasted, had their own range of dramatic statements. Then came the farewells, the break-up of the group at its largest and its disintegration as the family units made for home.

For each person present it was the same event but a different set of circumstances and spatial experiences. The picnic is long over, but it lives on in a space within me. I can replay my version, with or without cuts, any time and as often as I like, no matter what actual physical space I happen to be in. In that creative inner space I can use the actual event as a basis for a set of other versions, adding and changing any of the details that I choose. Even more, I am capable of imagining all that might have occurred both before and after the time I spent there. Though at the time I saw it all from within the group and as one of the group, in my inner viewing room I can see the scene from as many other angles as I please. In that space within you memories live and new themes and thoughts float up, offering an array of possibilities to be tested in the elusive search for the best possible form. I know that I have a virtual film studio inside me, in which I try out most of my creative ideas. In there I have seen, with my mind's eye, whole passages of movement ready to be tested on real bodies in real situations.

Martha Graham calls this space 'the inner landscape'.* Inside you, in your head space, your heart and gut space, live inherited and personal memories, dreams and nightmares, visions and fantasies, images and stories, pictures and possibilities of unseen things more fabulous than anything in reality. It is in this space that your originality lives. It is from within the peaks and valleys, the colours and the clouds of that landscape and dream space, that children play and our creativity springs.

---

* Martha Graham (1894–1991) was one of the most influential dancers and choreographers of the twentieth century.

It is so much about how you are in space, with your body in space. He gave you, or started to teach you, a sense of owning space. How to bring your presence in, not just about steps. Steps are steps but if there's no connection it doesn't mean anything.

You've got to fill that space with your presence. And I think that what he's able to do is make you feel good enough about yourself to be able to fill that space.

CHRISSIE KOLTAI

Back in the real world, some spaces and their accompanying atmospheres can be overpowering, diminishing you as your inner space contracts in comparison. At other times your inner space will expand in reaction to the environmental space you occupy. I have heard people describe how insignificant they feel in spaces like the Grand Canyon, while others feel magnified by their presence. I have never felt so energised and enlarged as when standing on a stage like the Bolshoi or the theatre at Epidaurus.

Acting theory talks endlessly of circumstances. So many circumstances are aspects of the concept of space. My own behaviour is modified many times a day as I pass from one kind of space, and the circumstances within it, to another. In familiar and loved surroundings my reactions reveal my ease and pleasure; but place me in unattractive, unfamiliar or formal circumstances and it will be a different me and my behaviour will tell a different story.

I have another understanding of space: space as nothingness. This conception of space has the potential for anything and everything, an emptiness waiting to be filled. It is the empty stage, the blank page, the bare canvas, the standing in the wings, the curtain about to rise, the darkened theatre, the before waiting for the after. It is the day before the first rehearsal. It is all the possibilities before they are defined and explored. Navigating this concept of space is no easy matter, but the finding of form—the giving of form in real space to our ideas and our dreams—is the creative priority of artists.

Direction

Direction is not simply a matter of such cardinal points as north and west. It can be any one of the infinite points in space surrounding you or to which you give attention. It can signify the line along which you move, look or gesture. It is the pathway you can make through space, whether forwards, sideways, backwards, curving or zigzag, or whether you travel in a direct or indirect manner. In the 'real' world your directional settings are pretty well absolute. In performance, however, they should also be relative to the audience or the camera.

The word 'direct' implies being full-on, straight, not round-about or interrupted, where the energy and movement of the whole body and its gestures are dedicated to the one point of focus and the one line of direction. The words 'indirect' and 'flexible' apply when, for example, the pathway towards an objective deviates by even the slightest degree or when much of the energy of a gesture or move is diffused and released in directions other than directly towards the focal point. There is a big contrast between the sense of functioning within the orbit of another person's spatial centre and that of being the radiating nucleus in our own spatial galaxy. These delicate distinctions and subtle definitions in our personal space are an invaluable part of the creative equipment. Only when space is seen and experienced as a totality of endless calibrations of angles and levels and directions emanating from the body and its various parts, can you expect an original, unpredictable, ingenious physical creation.

EXERCISE IN SPATIAL AWARENESS

Walk across the space, taking both direct and indirect pathways. Allow yourself to experience their differences. Then experiment with what it feels like to walk at different speeds, then perhaps pause for a moment or two.

Having felt these journeys across varying distances, add levels and start to pay attention to body shapes and your relationship to others, and to the space itself. Then transform the space into a stage with one wall as the audience. Become aware of your relationship with the audience and imagine what the audience sees and experiences.

> You can change the audience perspective by moving it from one wall to another. With each shift explore different positions within the space—upstage, downstage, centre stage etc and feel what it's like to be in each position relative to the audience.
>
> Also explore what part of you is revealed to the audience, different angles—front on, profile, back to the audience etc. Always keeping in mind your relationship to others in the space, and how you balance or complement the arrangement of bodies 'on stage'.
>
> JULIA COTTON

Levels

A study of space must include consideration of level—that is, how the heights and elevations vary of the people and objects that occupy the performing area. It is a powerful aesthetic and design element, giving dimension and variety to the stage picture. It is valuable in adding

steppingstone — a choreographed work based on Keith's life by Anca Frankenhaeuser. L to r Wendy Strehlow, Sonia Todd, Patrick Harding-Irmer, NIDA 2005.

status and strong contrast when staging group activity; it is an aid in highlighting moments of characterisation and storytelling; and is especially useful in achieving the right focus in climactic scenes.

This doesn't mean that the tallest and highest position always carries the greatest impact. It is more likely that whatever is the exception will draw the focus. Imagine that a scene has everyone standing in what are generally considered the strong positions on stage—high on the set and close to the centre—except for one figure, crouching or huddled low to the floor in what might normally be considered a weak spot. Focus will certainly swing to that single character, because they are the exception. Added to that, the expressive quality of that ambiguous position gives dramatic tension to the piece.

I respond to the height of a performing space as a calibrated distance from the bottom to the top, layer on layer of levels, each with its special quality, its own tonality. I love the sense, when raising or lowering, of entering new spatial areas, each with their own fresh view of the world and each with their own expressive key change.

Jesus Christ Superstar: Dir. Jim Sharman, Chor. Keith Bain, Capitol Theatre, Sydney, 1972.

Range

Range is the spatial property that indicates the amount of space the body uses. It can be the extent or scope of individual gestures or full-body movement. It is an aspect of flexibility and reach. It applies to the limits of mobility of which our limbs and body parts are capable. It can be a point of characterisation to consider, when playing an older person for example, the degree of articulation in joints such as knees, ankles, necks, wrists and shoulders.

Some people use space sparingly. For them, movement and gestures are contained and economic. Their energy is not diffused and their movement sets up no disturbance in the space around them. In contrast, there are those who seem to need a great deal of space to do even the simplest thing. They disturb the air they occupy and the space they travel through, and tend to unsettle the atmosphere around them. Naturally, in discussing differences such as these, we are referring to psychological as well as behavioural issues; but that fact applies to all considerations of movement in space.

Range is a strong element of group activity and of spacing, whether naturalistic, formal or stylised. It is a key feature of group activities like dancing. Each dance is characterised as much by its spatial range as by any other movement factor. But it is also a characteristic of blocking. One of the most valid justifications for teaching dance within a movement program is the mastery and appreciation of these qualities of space.

EXERCISE IN SPATIAL RANGE

First intimately explore the size of your 'own space', with both feet 'in place'. Then allow one leg to move. Next, share the space you are inhabiting with someone else without touching each other. Then move on to slowly expanding your available space to the whole room with as large movements as possible. In the end, let your space shrink back to your 'own space'. And finally slowly shrink that space until you are only moving internally within your own body.

Position

Of all the meanings for this word 'position', the important ones have to do with where one is on any performing area, and the significance of that spot in relation to the whole space and to the position of other people or things. Doris Humphrey, in her book, *The Art of Making Dances*, deals at length with the relative strengths and weaknesses of the range of positions on a stage.* She gives the centre, and both upstage and downstage corners, as examples of strong locations, and it is easy to see how many architectural and geometric forces are at play in giving power to whoever holds those positions. Most of her claims apply best when the performing space is empty of those elements of design and lighting that could serve to make an ordinarily weak spot significant.

I love watching good directors moving and placing actors so that focus, forever changing, is always clear; and space generally, and position specifically, become dramatic elements at the service of the play. It is easier to test the effectiveness of positioning when looking at the stage from out front than it is when you are part of the stage action yourself. There are stage-wise performers whose sensitivity to placement ensures that they never mask another actor or allow themselves to be masked or outpositioned by a fellow player. These are the ones who will 'feel' the need for a spatial adjustment either to take the focus or yield it to someone else. They have an appreciation from within of how their positioning is being registered by the audience. The really accomplished performer is as aware of the potential of the stage spaces he is *not* using as he is of the spot he now occupies.

The same concerns about placement for the cast apply to elements of the set. Audiences would be amazed at the time it can take in rehearsal to find the perfect spot and angle for the sofa, the dining table, the piano so that no important stage business is obscured, none of the cast is disadvantaged and the set doesn't win over the players. A great deal

---

* Doris Humphrey and Barbara Pollack. A Dance Horizons Book, 1959.

We did an extended exercise quite early in our training, the importance of perspective and relationship of bodies to other bodies in the space. This has informed my work especially in terms of seeing the whole, being aware of the whole picture and the relationship to the viewer.

PAUL BLACKWELL

of artifice and aesthetic judgment is often needed in the positioning of the people and the furniture to create the effect of naturalism.

Here I have two very strong preferences. One is to avoid over-using the centre of the performing space. In too many productions I see whole sequences of scenes played out centre stage. I accept that stage centre is a powerful spot but its potency can be weakened by over-use. Keep it for the big moments and find the variety and the nuances that are offered elsewhere. My second preference is to avoid full-frontal encounters and instead angle the bodies and set pieces to give a rich three-dimensional quality. By regularly playing position games, placing yourself in different locations within a given space, you can experience what each position offers. Try placing yourself at an entrance, against the back wall or dead centre; sit at the very front of the space or as far as possible from other people; stand in front of someone, close at their side or directly behind them; or find a level higher or lower than everyone else.

Angle and orientation

Both angle and orientation apply to how you relate to the audience, to another actor, or to anything within your surroundings. It is easy to set up experiments that will help you to become sensitive to the meanings and powers associated with such variations as standing front-on to a fellow actor, then comparing that with any manner of indirect angling of the body. The same piece of shared dialogue spoken in different spatial orientations can yield up extraordinary subtleties when these possibilities are investigated.

Actors new to the game allow themselves to be trapped into the front-to-front, eyeball-to-eyeball orientation—I call it missionary-position acting. To make it worse, they tend also to present themselves in profile to the audience, who are bound to find that this two-dimensional

Drew Forsythe and cast in *The Venetian Twins*: Dir. John Bell, Chor. Keith Bain, Sydney Theatre Company 1979.

position makes body language difficult to read and the whole scene more difficult to hear. Clever uses of the myriad of body angles are an expressive way to indicate status and formality, familiarity and the degree of intimacy, tension, and provide variety and atmosphere.

Different media require different a sensitivity to determine the most appropriate angle for each occasion. Performing on a proscenium stage, for instance, asks for a different awareness of stage and audience to a thrust space or theatre-in-the-round. Film and television make other demands of body angling and orientation to achieve their full power. Added to that is the need for the actor to be sensitive to these qualities in close-up, long-shot and full body shot.

For me a great part of the joys of viewing a free-standing sculpture is to register the changes in what I take in as I move around the work and encounter the statements it offers me from every angle and distance. A single work, if it is good enough, will yield up hundreds of qualities and points of interest. The same sensibility can be explored when relating to someone onstage.

Distance

Distance is a quality of space that speaks strongly for an actor and yet it is the one that actors seem not to consciously exploit. In body language terms, the distance between us and another person or object is a clue to relationships, intentions, emotional and psychological states. Socially, there are distances that, while acceptable for certain degrees of familiarity, are intrusive or unacceptable for others. Social convention dictates zones or territories that are distinguished by the distances considered appropriate for, say, meeting people for the first time, greeting old and dear friends, formal introductions in formal surroundings. The adjusting of distance to resist the invasion of our private space is an eloquent move that needs no words.

So much of the potential revelation of the moods, wants and denials between people is expressible simply by manipulating distance, including the acts of approaching, separating, parting, passing, stopping and circling. Powerful statements can be made by the most surprising means. For instance, closer-and-closer does not necessarily create as strong an effect of attraction as further-and-further-away. There are no rules in this matter. The context determines the effect. People get closer to fight and argue as well as to kiss and cuddle. The further apart people are, the richer can be the currents of feeling that electrify the distance between them.

Distance, like most of the elements of space, can be a useful tool in the processes of stylisation. It most certainly plays a role in establishing the physical detailing of an actor's characterisation and their interplay with the other members of the cast. I witnessed a delicious detail of space use in the behaviour of two young lovers sharing a table at a coffee shop. Until their arrival, the rest of us at our breakfasts were relating to our partners in a comfortable and casual way. The lovers, however, entered, still pressed together from the night before, both still inside the one bubble of hot, intimate space. How they managed to negotiate the crowded tables while remaining stuck so tightly to one another made their locomotion through the cafe a wonder to watch. Each was a

Keith and Helen Lisle in rehearsal for Concerto Grosso—Vivaldi. Chor Keith Bain, Art Gallery of NSW, early 1960s.

half of a single unit as they manoeuvred to a spot in a quiet corner. When that structure broke to allow them to sit opposite each other, they set up a magnetic field between them that pulled them towards each other until they met at every possible body part both above and below the table-top. The detail I loved the most was when their cappuccinos were served and they sensuously invaded each other's territory by reaching across to feed the other or help themselves to the chocolate-covered froth from the other's cup—all done with slow strokes of their long-stemmed spoons. The closeness of the two, the forward curve of their bodies across the table, the symmetry of the total design; and other details, like the language of their eye contact, made up of alternating direct and indirect gazes, and their disregard of everything around them, projected a wave of intimacy through the entire cafe.

Design is an elaborate spatial concept. It has application to several aspects of staging such as the shaping of individual bodies, the arrangement of bodies and objects within a defined space, and the counter-balancing of groups and bodies in static positions or locomotor activity, in relation to the set and the audience. Constant regard for the look and the picture, far from having only aesthetic responsibilities, can make a visual statement of the meaning, style, atmosphere and intention of the piece being presented.

Symmetry and Asymmetry

Basic to any study of spatial design are explorations of the principles of symmetry and asymmetry. Symmetry demands a state of perfect balance on either side of a central line. This perfection in the proportion and shaping of the total design is both its strength and its weakness. Its properties of stability, equilibrium, precision and uniformity are symbols of control, order, and organisation. Judging by the way some of my acquaintances choose their clothes, set out their garden, place their furniture and prefer their theatre, symmetry is the chief quality determining their idea of beauty.

When I ask students to create symmetrical designs with individual bodies or groups of bodies, with or without props and objects in a space, it interests me to discover how quickly they move from an early excitement in the power and comfort of their creations to sensing how restrictive is the dramatic potential. Try it for yourself. Being part of a symmetrical design leaves you with the sensation of having lost a sense of yourself as you conform to the pattern. The form wins over the other dramatic elements. You might find it hard to be funny, tragic or to be effectively human. However, it is a valuable theatrical device and only requires awareness of what it does well, what are its limits and how you fit within them.

Doris Humphrey, in her bluntly expressed checklist for aspiring choreographers, writes that symmetry is lifeless and two-dimensional.* This is a sweeping statement, but the truth in it must be recognised. Each example of symmetrical form, by being perfect and complete, gives no promise of change: it is comparatively passive and un-dynamic. If it is drama you want, if excitement and unpredictability, personality, transition and innovation are what turn you on, then asymmetry will provide you with the dynamic range you need.

That said, symmetry on a grand scale can be stunning and highly emotional. Think of a royal wedding, the Nuremburg Rallies, the opening ceremonies of the Olympic Games... Finales of musicals and ballets are all symmetrical knockouts— more superhuman than human.

---

*   *The Art of Making Dance*, Doris Humphrey and Barbara Pollack. A Dance Horizons Book, 1959.

Focus

In theatrical terms focus is any centre of interest, attention or activity throughout the unfolding of a piece. The participants are not fully engaged in every moment of the action nor for them is every moment equally important. The focus, like a football, passes from person to person, action to action, rising and falling in intensity and significance, from the instant the piece begins to its closing moments.

Good performers are concerned not just with their own role. They are generous enough to yield focus to the appropriate player, then assume it once more—but only when it is important to do so—and to support it each time it is taken up again by someone else. An insensitive performer is so self-occupied that they have little understanding of where the focus shifts and changes and, as a result, is more often in competition with the play's focus than supportive of it.

But focus can also apply to the power of a performer to regulate and direct their senses so that the direction of their attention is immediately apparent. And that means attention with all the senses. Focus could just as easily be a matter of a touch, taste, smell or sound. You may shut your eyes to intensify your mental focus and sharpen the workings of the other senses. You focus inwardly when you are dredging up a memory, trying to visualise something not present in your surroundings, thinking about what might happen, concentrating on how you are feeling, or working out a problem in your head.

I believe that few of us are aware of the number of times that, even in ordinary conversation, we change from a state of directed focus to one of de-focus. The physical changes that distinguish the two states are so small it is hard to credit how clearly they register with somebody watching, even in the back row of a big theatre. Yet they are responsible for revealing the strongest evidence of our acts of thinking, daydreaming or remembering. You de-focus from your surrounds when you send your thoughts backwards and forward in time or when your mind revisits old environments and imagines new ones. As I sit here, I feel myself de-focusing each time I search in my head for a better word, a fresh thought. Not only am I aware of the way my eyes disengage themselves, the better to do my thinking, but I feel them turn upwards or downwards; and then, the minute that internal process is over, back I go to a positive focus and get on with the job.

In performance, people tend to lock eyes throughout their conversations as though the characters never have to search for words, get their argument together, recall names, facts and places or visualise the stories they are telling. In a formal situation

John Howard and Susan Lyons in *Nicholas Nickelby*. Dir. Richard Wherrett, Movement Keith Bain, Sydney Theatre Company 1983.

you may maintain that concentrated focus on someone you are meeting, but it is a mark of an easy relationship when you can relax and look away or continue unrelated business while chatting. Worst of all is the use of eye and head focus that has no corresponding mental attention. Real focus is active concentration, a reading of the situation, a genuine reaction to the information being offered, moment by moment. It is not just seeing what is to be seen but interpreting and assessing what is significant and what can be ignored.

EXERCISE FOR BODY-MEMORY, FOCUS AND SPATIAL AWARENESS

Keith would give the students several instructions: 'You are late for work'; 'You are at the airport to meet someone with a birthmark on their right cheek: find him.' 'Adjust your clothing; you are looking at a studio to rent: check it out.' During each activity Keith claps as an indication for the students to freeze and hold their position. He then gives instructions that on his clap: 'You will turn to someone who called your name; gesture towards someone without touching them; touch someone; make really strong physical contact.' In each of these positions students must make note of where they are in relation to the space and to everybody around them, as well as to the kinetic detail of their own body shape. In this exercise students also experience different points and depths of focus and give their peripheral vision a good workout. Keith gave each position a number so that they could be repeated in order, and through the whole exercise he would ask the students to go backwards and forwards through the different positions and then add another.

Keith talked about the 'body-brain' and told his students to trust their bodies to remember and to take them back. Students also report that they could 'feel' each of the positions and the atmosphere their imaginations had produced with each scenario. They even found they developed pathways to each position so that the transitions became as familiar as the positions themselves. This made the students appreciate the importance and relevance of spatial awareness, focus and body memory in a fun way. A week or two later Keith might surprise them by asking them to repeat these positions. This exercise was often given early in the course, sometimes even in the first class, and it quickly reassured the students that they were equally capable, that there were no right and wrong ways to do it and that it did not require technical skill. It does, however, serve the dual purpose of making the actors more sensitive to their surroundings and at the same time heightens their own body awareness.

JULIA COTTON

Time

Time is the reference against which we measure our journey through each set of circumstances, each stage of our journey through life. For some of us the present is the obsession, for others the future and all it promises or threatens; while for a few, the past will become their chief preoccupation and benchmark for evaluating all present experience. Think of all those Chekhovian characters, caught in the quicksand of their past, who deal so poorly with the present and whose future is so unsure. For the actor the real significance lies in the human, richly subjective, highly personal interaction with time. How you put time to use or are used by time, to what degree you indulge in time or are at its mercy, are some of the many ways in which we are differentiated from each other, and how our motivations and behaviour are explained to others. The measuring of time is a matter of context, mood and circumstance. Actors tend to overlook a gold mine of information about inner life and overt behaviour when they ignore an examination of these attitudes. The following thoughts may help give depth to the characterisation process and find clues to behaviour patterns and physicality.

We have all felt those occasions when time stands still and when time is flying; when it goes too fast and when it drags and weighs us down. There are those whose success in life is based on an ability to tame it, bringing order to their existence. Being unable to manage it can become the main factor in the chaos that people's lives can become. I am a congenitally early person and am in agony if there is the slightest possibility I might be late. No one makes me angrier than the person who is not only late for everything but has no conscience or consciousness of the effect their lateness has on others.

Examples abound of people who are the first to comment, offer advice, or respond in an emergency. I am sure you know, too, those who are the last to do any of the above, those who never have time, who are slow but don't know it or are slow and do; who take half as long, or twice as long, as anyone else, regardless of the task. Morning may be the time of some people's greatest energy, the afternoon a killer for others, and night, for many I know, is the big time, the only time. The characters you play are exactly the same.

As an artist you are lucky. You can bend time to your own ends. You can speed up action or slow it down; you can cut or segue, replace a natural rhythm with a metrical one; you can jump to any point of time and make time submit to your creative needs. You can encapsulate years of real time in a few clever minutes. You can range backwards and forwards through what in reality is a perfect continuum.

Yet we Western creators are more cautious with our experiments with time than with either space or energy. I have witnessed ritualistic enactments in Bali that lasted through the night till the very moment the sun rose out of the sea, illuminating the scatter of petals, the marks in the dust of the dancers' footprints and the few drops of blood from a sacrificed chicken. Butoh suspends time, slowing down both action and reaction, allowing each unfolding moment to be savoured, or suffered, and for the emotional content to be magically distilled. As Westerners we have to fight impatience at many non-Western performances which ask us to accept another culture's use of time. But the rewards are worth everything. Time to look deeply, time to notice the slightest change, time to be aware of the passing of time. To dare to do nothing, stretch time till it nearly breaks, is almost the bravest thing a modern Western artist can attempt.

Western audiences have become expert at coping with short takes and quick cuts in film and television, and are used to action-packed, high-energy productions in which these elements seem more important than hearing every word or appreciating subtlety of detail and style. It's good to remind yourself that time is not always best expressed by how much action can be fitted into every second. It is worth remembering too, that each person present has a different time experience of that event. On an occasion as

Keith Bain should be declared a National Treasure... he has influenced generations of Australian actors, designers and directors with his striving for physical and organic truth, commitment and precision in all performance moments.
GALE EDWARDS

innocent as a family celebration, the varied ages, moods, histories and personalities of the individuals at the gathering will produce differing perceptions of time passing. The behaviour of the older relatives, the newly-weds, the teenagers and the babies, the hosts and the guest-of-honour will reflect their divergent perception of time.

Time as a major element of movement has its own sub-categories:

Timing

Timing is judgment of the right moment and the right speed to achieve the most effective performance. It can refer to the delivery of a line or word in the dialogue; it can be the sensing of the perfect moment for a piece of stage business to begin, continue and end. Poor timing has proved to be a terminal deficiency for many an actor. Good timing is part of the craft of every fine performer and is an absolutely essential ingredient in the playing of comedy. A clever comedian can bring the house down with ordinary material by timing his delivery in response to his feel of the audience. He knows when to make them wait and when to take them by surprise, when to move and when to be still. Timing is a gift that will never be granted to performers who work in a vacuum, who lack antennae to pick up the audience vibration.

Timing is also about appreciating the speeds at which words are spoken and movements are made, not simply a matter of fast or slow but of knowing when acceleration, deceleration, hesitation or sudden attack, consistency or variance, is what will produce the preferred outcome. It can be as difficult to teach these skills to people not naturally gifted, as it is to teach pitch to a tone-deaf singer. Nevertheless, sensitivity to these time elements can be improved through discussion and evaluation sessions like workshops and master classes.

Public speakers and political figures seek to create their biggest effects through the use of emphatic timing. A most terrifyingly successful example of this was Hitler. On the public platform his punctuated and practised oratory and declamatory gestures mesmerised millions of his countrymen in speeches which drove them into a state of hysterical acceptance. Watching our Parliament on television, by contrast, is generally a dull experience, because the majority of parliamentarians have no command of timing techniques. Even their best statements miss their target; others are so transparently contrived that the effect is bombastic.

Phrasing

I wasn't surprised to find that my dictionary limited its definitions of 'phrase' to its application in music and speech. No mention of phrasing in movement and dance at all. But phrasing is as distinctive a mark of a fine mover as it is of a great singer, instrumentalist, conductor or dancer. It is evident in how Judy Dench enlivens and enriches any text she delivers: it is how Sinatra, Ella Fitzgerald and Aretha Franklin bring meaning to songs that other people merely sing; it is through sensitivity to the phrase that the dancers whom we most admire personalise the choreography, put their own signature on it and claim it as their own.

EXERCISE FOR EXPLORING QUALITIES OF MOVEMENT AND PHRASING

This exercise is done with chairs. Find ten different positions, on or touching a chair, positions that can be repeated in order and in reverse order. Then move through these positions in a continuous flow of movement or fragmented by sharp changes from one to another. Repeat the exercise with music, experimenting with styles of music from classical to rock—and everything in between. Also experiment with the transitions between the positions, change between continuous and sharp staccato movements. The moving within the musical structure introduces the additional element of time into the task, particularly the phrasing of time.

JULIA COTTON

Unison

Unison can be a way of moving bodies through identical patterns in space but, equally, it can be a matter of having two or more people using time in simultaneous fashion. When well judged, the technique can multiply the power of speed and timing of a single body by the number of bodies involved, as well as being a tool in the process of stylisation. It generates a range of effects, from discipline, harmony and unity through to images of subjection, mechanisation and conformity. But only when all the participants maintain the rhythm and rate. Unison is not a naturalistic device. It can be considered as the parallel in time to symmetry in space.

To move in true unison with others is not easy. So many controls and so much awareness are necessary to achieve it. The ability to move in accord with other people depends on a complicated parcel of sensitivities including coordination, peripheral vision, spatial definition, rhythmic control, quick reflexes, empathy and unselfishness. Experimenting with someone else under a variety of circumstances will reveal how difficult this can be.

It is always the exception that catches the eye and it is rare for there to be no exceptions when unison is demanded. My eye is drawn like a magnet to irregularities—that swan in *Swan Lake* whose leg goes too high, destroying the effect the others are working so hard to achieve. In your work you will no doubt have the experience of working with performers who are temperamentally incapable of submerging their own sense of time and phrasing in the group.

Counterpoint

Counterpoint is another term from music and refers to a combination of two or more sets of contrasting movement patterns and timings. It may apply to one person functioning in simultaneous, but differing, time elements, such as walking in a regular, sustained rhythm accompanied by arrhythmic, staccato, head flicks and rapid, vibratory, hand gestures. It is a technique that creates a textured, layered effect of time and space design. Savouring the coexistent elements, and appreciating the effect its unity creates, is similar to appreciating the full force of an orchestral work while distinguishing the inner riches of the instrumental strands. It is not only a theatrically effective factor in formal and stylised theatre but gives dimension and colour to a variety of commonplace activities inside the most naturalistic productions. Group scenes in realistic drama can be enlivened and humanised when the overall atmosphere is compounded by a richly contrapuntal blend of each character's use of time—not accidental but achieved through careful choices.

Canon

Canon is yet one more musical form that has a movement parallel. Musically it is a round in which the same theme is successively introduced, as in part-songs like *Three Blind Mice*. Translated into movement the sequence becomes its own accompaniment, with each participant performing the same pattern but in a different part of that sequence.

So interlocked are the space-time-energy trinity that I could have mentioned these last three categories under one heading. I could also have dealt with counterpoint and canon in any discussion of ways to develop, elaborate or modify, as in music, a movement sequence.

Random timing

We live by chance, by accident, and coincidences are as likely as certainties. The 'when' of life is as fortuitous and haphazard as the 'why' and the 'how'. But each accidental moment, when lifted from its context and framed by a stage can be seen to have an order, a design and a time value. Revealing the accidents of life in an artistic frame of reference is not best achieved by accidental means. The organising of adventitious action in an opera, play or film can be a painstaking logistical exercise in timing and design. Nevertheless, random timing is a legitimate theatrical technique, comparable to random sound-making in music and singing, random spatial patterns in dance and random drippings, smudgings and scribblings in painting. In these and other examples there is often a degree of plan and control. But the random element in the arts, with its qualities of spontaneity and improvisational freedom, is an artistic practice of the most exciting kind.

Rhythm

Rhythm is always a tough nut to crack in the teaching of Movement. Many folk give themselves credit for having a sense of rhythm, but, when put to the test, find that theirs is more aural than the sensual, visceral, muscular experience it should be. Fifty percent of each fresh intake of students, when asked to walk in time to a regular drum beat will be irregular in some way. Some will be aware they are unable to synchronise with the beat. Others will be content, unconscious of the discrepancy between what they are doing, what others are doing, and what was asked of them in the first place.

There are three clear kinds of rhythm to be dealt with in performance: *metrical rhythm*, *dramatic rhythm* and that *rhythmic flow* which character-ises the underlying pulse that gives life and distinction to artists and the artworks they create. The first of these applies most frequently to those measured phrases of weak and strong accents that you can find in music. These are often the rhythms that you can count. Many of the popular dance forms are characterised by their distinctive rhythms, even when their time signatures are identical. Waltzes, minuets, polonaises may have the same number of beats to the bar as rhumbas, mambos and cha chas, gavottes and polkas. But their patterns of rhythmic accents differ, not just in mathematical terms but in essential subtleties that lead, when you move into them, to all sorts of delicious variations of deportment and projection, body stylings, speeds, footwork, space patterning and personality.

Dramatic rhythm has another appeal altogether. Our emotional states and moods produce changes in our body rhythms that are not mathematically calculable, consistent or intellectually designed and are individual representations of your inner life. The body rhythms produced by a state of panic contrast with those expressed when you are furiously angry, excitedly expectant or bored to sobs. Even when experiencing a similar emotional state, no two people will register them in the same rhythmic response. Add your own list of emotional conditions and you should be able to visualise an astonishing range of expressive rhythms chiefly indicated through varying gestures, tensions and shapes.

But there is another view of rhythm, a complex mix of qualities involving every aspect of movement that is described as *rhythmic flow*. It is the way each of us does things, suavely or clumsily, efficiently or lacking in coordination. It applies to all our activities at work or play, on the dance floor or making love. In some of these situations you will find the rhythm that solves the problem and reveals you at your best. The skills that defeat us, and the activities that take us longest to master, are mostly the ones with rhythms you can't absorb.

My dictionaries' definitions of rhythm are all about regular and recurring accents, more often relative to music and words than to movement. This other rhythm, this rhythmic flow, includes all that and a great deal more. It is about the ups and downs of our prevailing moods, our dominant and recessive dynamics, the particular speed of our walk, the space we affect, the scope of our personalities, the control of our temperament, the outward effect on our behaviour of our emotions, energies and thought processes, and the degree of our tension and relaxation. It is one of the hardest qualities to define, and is applied not only to defining us humans but in summing-up a painting, a play, a novel or any artwork. The closest I can get to it is to describe it as the way the elements flow or clash together—the ultimate coordination of all the qualities, the flow of the chemical mix of all the ingredients. We need adjectives, not beats, to express the nature of this kind of rhythm.

Speed

The speed with which we move reveals heaps of information about our nature and identity. My thesaurus gives as synonyms for 'speed' words like swiftness, velocity, quickness, haste, alacrity, hurry, rush, promptness. The definition of 'slow' includes slack, unhurried, lagging, tardy, inertial. The range between the two is enormous not just in physical terms but also in their psychological implications. Not to know that you are, for instance, a slow person by nature, can make judgment a tricky affair when considering details of character-playing. If you are a quick person you may need a lot of help to gain control of slow movement. Controlling the skills of acceleration and deceleration is one more useful theatrical technique, along with the capacity to distinguish between a moment in time and duration in time.

EXERCISE FOR ACCELERATION AND DECELERATION

This exercise, although simple, is also quite challenging. Students form a circle equidistant apart all facing in the same, anti-clockwise, direction. They are then instructed to start slowly walking forward, maintaining the distance between each other at all times, gradually increasing the speed until they are running. They run as fast as they can, still keeping the distance, and then start to slow down, until they all arrive at a stop at the same time. This requires a considerable amount of concentration and control.

By experiencing the associated feelings attached to different speeds, urgency, anticipation etc, the student connects to more than the technical aspect of acceleration and deceleration. They also experience very clearly when they are in harmony with each other and when they are at odds: it is quite usual for some to be impatient, to find it hard to maintain the gradual acceleration and deceleration. It also gives students another scale of reference. Speeding things up and slowing them down can be used both in creating material and in practical ways applied to rehearsal and performance.

JULIA COTTON

EXERCISE IN RHYTHM AND WORKING MOMENT BY MOMENT

From lying on the floor completely relaxed, the students suddenly, without moving, become alert. Then like an animal, they move an increment at a time towards getting up. Keith would get them to pause at some point and then precisely reverse the sequence back to the floor; he may get them to repeat this a couple of times. He would then instruct the students to change from a staccato rhythm to a continuous flow. He taught them to appreciate each moment on the journey by making them aware of the complexities inherent in even the smallest movement.

JULIA COTTON

Energy/Weight/Dynamics

Each of these words—'energy', 'weight', 'dynamics'—is related to the others, but each has its special implications. For instance, the word 'dynamics' sparks off ideas of colour, texture and flavour. It also brings up contrasting images like rough or creamy, jagged or liquid. It allows the representation of moods, atmospheres and personal movement in tones and contrasting shades of strength and intensity. It awakens images of emotion as colours, sometimes deepening, sometimes fading and flickering, hanging in the air or glowing deep inside. It reminds me of the pressures of my own feelings, of my temperament and the range of forces behind my gestures as I constrain or release my inner life.

Energy is *us*. It is a personal, not a cosmic property, which differs in each of us. We move and live because of it and are dead when that life force shuts down. Our individual ways of using it, its intensities and qualities, make it one of the clearest points of differentiation between ourselves and other people; and on that basis alone provides an area of special study.

It is too easy for energy to be valued as simply a measure of physical effort. Energy manifests itself in different ways. For example, intellectual, sensual, sexual, spiritual and emotional energies are all a big part of human nature. We are strongly identified by the energy levels of our responses to appetite and enthusiasm, indifference and hatred; ambitions, frustrations and the obstacles that stand between us and what we want. Not to appreciate the richness of these other energy fields puts a limit on deeper searching into characterisation and the techniques of stylisation.

As I was discovering the various Movement theories, my literal mind immediately confined 'weight' to a concern for all that was heavy, full of effort and slow. It was a great day when I applied to myself the advice I gave my students: 'Avoid generalisations and seek out specifics in every aspect of your work.' First I considered weight's opposite meanings and implications. I began to see weight no longer as an absolute but as a range and a continuum. Weight revealed itself as essentially related to non-weight, and to all that is lightest, most sustained and effortless, as much as it is to heaviness. Energy, when seen also as lack of, or absence of, power, ceases to be a general thing and invites a million specific possibilities. Secondly, I made the quality being considered the central point on a line graph, and then tried to visualise all the gradations that lie on the spectrum between the extremes of positives and negatives.

Robert Grubb and cast of *The Threepenny Opera*: Dir. George Whaley, Chor. Keith Bain, NIDA 1987.

This process has been a big help in showing what dynamic range exists and keeps me from making narrow definitions, and choices.

Our movement language generally, and the intimate field of kinaesthetics particularly, lacks the vocabulary to describe and distinguish between the flavours of feeling, and the infinity of inner and outer reactions that make movement the universal and basic activity of life. Richly sensory things are impossible to describe. How could you describe what apple pie tastes like to someone who has never eaten an apple? How could you describe to anyone who had never experienced an orgasm what it feels like? One tool to attempt this impossibility is to make a list of examples—situations, verbs, adjectives and images in an attempt to indicate the range and extent each sensory experience can encompass.

Energy

Most actors when encouraged to invest their work with a richer 'energy', respond by doing and saying everything faster, louder, stronger, and with greater forcefulness and urgency. This is a legitimate response, but what about richer feeling, thinking and sensing? Is it not possible to get closer to the essence of both personal and character studies by investigating the emotional, sensual, sexual, intellectual, spiritual and nervous energy levels as well as the physical ones?

Every visit I make to the nursing home to see my old mother is a revelation of energy functioning in as many different combinations, and on as many levels, as there are occupants, but with physical energy being least in evidence. Few of the bodies in the beds and wheelchairs register any movement or physical animation. But the evidence of their intellectual and emotional energy reveals itself in the discerning focus, the brightness, quickness and knowingness in their eyes, and in the smiles and changing expressions in response to the pleasure and pain with which their limited world presents them. The most acute and active mind can be seen at work in the most inert frame; and conversely, bodies, still capable of mobility, may be home to a mind long since come to a standstill. There are frequent outbursts of energetic physical and emotional response, out of all proportion to what has provoked them, and it is heartbreaking to witness the effort and tension at work in an old body responding to the frantic energy of an old mind bewildered by an environment it can no longer interpret. One lesson I have learned from these visits is that if effort is the result of energy, then it is not always the brilliant academic mind that is fired by the highest levels of intellectual energy. Rather, it is the slow mind and the mind that struggles to grasp simple ideas and confusing situations. The outlay of energy that a stroke victim must expend to move his walking frame the tiny distance from the chair to the bed might not be much less than that which an athlete gives to his game.

At the other end of the spectrum, babies and youngsters are a fascinating study because they illustrate, in a vividly primal and spontaneous manner, so many different intensities of energy use, so many categories and manifestations of energy at work, and a richer range of dynamics than often survive into adulthood. One of the greatest characteristics of youth is surely that of generating more energy than can be contained in mere walking and economic movement; of having energy to burn, to waste, to use up in unnecessary but irresistibly pleasurable movement.

I have heard experts confidently claim that the body possesses a single energy centre, precisely placed by some in the gut, by others in the solar plexus, by others again in the region of the diaphragm—and that the whole vital business of physical expression depends on the capacity of an actor to tap into their animal energy source and release it through the body. My experience has been that we have a variety of such centres, including the head, the chest (especially the region of the breast-bone) even the bowels and the genitals. It is this experience that confirms my belief that several forms of energy are at work in me and that the energy supporting me when I am involved with hard physical labour is not the same as supplies the fuel for my temper and enthusiasm, my sensual and sexual appetite or the intellectual struggles such as the one I am having at this moment trying to find the best way to say what I am saying now. (I am noticing how de-energised my main body and trunk have become while my brain is doing its gymnastics.)

Emotional Energy

All the characters you will play are differentiated by degrees of emotional energy. Just think how deadened and covered is the expression of emotion in some individuals and how volatile and close to the surface is that of others. In any one play, think how the pressure of your character's emotional state constantly changes in relation to the circumstances, how much or how little it takes for the emotional taps to be turned on, and whether the flow is a trickle or a flood. Think also how contradictory are the levels of emotional energy in a single individual: how a violent explosion can erupt from an apparently trivial cause; and then, with a slight change of context, what different readings will be measured on the same person's Richter scale of emotions.

To play any character you need to know the levels of your own emotional states so that you can prepare for the differences between your own nature and the inner life of the character you are playing. Not having knowledge of the readings on your own emotional scale is a bad way to set out to understand and represent the inner life of someone else. If you have never realised how animated (above average) or how phlegmatic (below average) you are, you are likely to over- or under- play the truth of any role you play.

Nervous energy

To work subtlety with emotional energy you need great discernment and relaxation. Otherwise that bugbear nervous energy takes over. Nervous energy can be a manifestation of fear of failure, determination to be better than everyone else, or just plain self-consciousness. Apart from the forced quality that nervous energy produces, its worst effect is the way it depletes your energy resource, wearing you down and using up your reserves.

On my many travels to overseas drama schools, I have been made aware of the differences between one school and another, and one nationality and another, in the value placed on the portrayal and registering of emotion. For citizens of one culture it is normal enough to release strong personal feelings without restraint, while another society's disapproval of emotional display demands that much of what is felt must be buried deep. These cultural attitudes are reflected in what we see on the stages and screens of different countries. The acting of many of those trained in, say, the Slavic systems of Eastern Europe is more overt in its volatile emotional content and expressiveness than we encourage in Anglo-Saxon training. Here the emotion is less a primary element of performance technique, and more a secondary result of the degree of our success or failure to get what we want.

In the Slavic example, the emotions seem to live close to the surface, ready to spill over, from just behind the eye and the lip, just under the skin and where the tiniest of impulses can activate the shoulders, torso, hands and face into uninhibited expressiveness. In the majority of Australian schools, by contrast, playing *the emotion* is a cardinal sin. I am not stating a preference here. In response to its cultural restraints, Western theatre can produce an underplayed, highly charged, implicit-rather-than-explicit acting style that carries great impact in its revelation of passionate states.

The following may sound an embarrassingly cute image, but I offer it to assist you in making more accurate judgments when asked for 'a bit less of this or a bit more of that' emotional reaction to a moment in a production. Imagine an emotional control panel on your chest with as many knobs representing individual qualities as are important, and to turn these up or down until a match between your own and the character's levels of energy is established. It can have the effect of turning up or down the flame, the electric current, the pressure gauge—however one wishes to think of it. Imagine too that there are ten possible settings on the control panel to help in giving range to each variety of energy. Consider also that you are made up of specific combinations of energy forms such as sensory, sexual, spiritual, kinetic and intellectual, as well as the physical, nervous and emotional ones. By adjusting the settings of these imaginary controls you can bring refreshing variation and detail to your characterisations. For example, if you have high levels of, say, physical and emotional energy—demonstrative, tactile, excitable, vivacious and eager—but your present task is playing the role of someone phlegmatic, frigid, listless and impassive, try resetting your *thermostat* to a lower level to experience more accurately the reduced levels of energy pressure experienced by your new character. It staggers me how miming the setting of these dials at different levels succeeds in changing the body's inner state.

Sensory energy

We are attached to our worlds by means of the senses. My world is special to me and different from yours, largely through my sensory appetite (a yearning for the richness of the experiences gained from the five senses) and my sensory energy (a mutual, and active engagement with the experiences of the physical world). My perception, my powers of perceiving, can be defined as my mental grasp of the life around me through the workings of my senses. We are filled and fired by the shapes, the colours, the textures, the flavours, the sounds, the feel, the smells of all that become the things we love or hate, tolerate or ignore. The energy behind our sensuous responses is what makes us the gourmets, or gourmands, of life and living.

Sexual Energy

Sexual energy is another key category, with the same enormous range on the lust graph from overmastering sexual appetite through the subtler stages to frigidity and austerity, innocence and purity. All the five senses play a big part in the sexual story both in experiencing real life and in the portrayal of states of desire in performance.

Sex is too primary and dominant an element in theatre not to be openly acknowledged and discussed. In every corner of the natural world, the energy generated by the sex drive is irrepressible. It is one of the most basic forms of communication. Because of society's checks on the practical fulfilment of our desires, the pressure of our sexual appetite remains pretty high and consistent, so that sexual pursuit and its obstacles is a subject of universal curiosity and the one with which the theatre artist has most frequently to deal.

Given this level of audience identification, it is not easy to avoid over-use of stereotypic stances, hip and pelvic thrusts, leers and pouting, hands-on-hips acting, tongue flicks and crotch-rubbings. We see them so often presented in performance as demonstrations, rather than true evidence, of sexual stirrings and invitations. I hesitate to offer an alternative list of clichés, but the language of passion is worth examining for its more varied and individual manifestations. However, it is important to be aware of the windows of the body that we open to transmit and receive messages: the duration, heat and directness of the looks and focus; the play of distance and the invasion of intimate space.

As important as the movement of sexual energy between the characters is the sexual relationship into which the audience enters with the performers. To be able to represent rich sexual attractiveness, to release and transmit that appeal, to exert the pull of that magnetism on other people, to give off a sort of sexual call or scent, to raise the sexual temperature and envelop the space (and everyone in it) with a palpably fecund atmosphere, is not something you can simulate. Some lucky people radiate it. Some don't know they have it, and it

Judy Davis and Dawn Blay in *Once in a Lifetime*: Dir. Richard Wherrett, Movement Keith Bain, NIDA 1977.

is not automatically present in handsome faces and beautiful bodies. Neither is it the special domain of the young and lusty. It is a difficult area to teach, and, I suspect, to learn. Like a lot of things in the art of performance, there are no codified rules for sexual attraction but it can at least be a point of reference in almost every Movement or acting class you take. The release of sexual energy is one of the elements within, say, all lessons on alignment, space, time and dynamic explorations, isolations, gesture, dance, sensory and emotional studies, observational analysis, centring, focus, release points and especially, experiments in transmitting, receiving and inviting through space.

The expression of love, lust and sexual energy is too easily generalised. To help us remain specific, the same old checklists need be consulted. What is the context? Does it allow an undisguised revelation of feeling or to what degree must it be monitored and modified? What features or mannerisms of our partner are a special turn-on? Which bit would you love to touch? Are you drawn to the hair, the laugh, the throat, the colouring, the lip, the chest, the shyness or the boldness of the eye? How experienced and confident or untried and timid? Over-sexed or under-sexed? How is your reading on the graph from one to ten? From under control to hot as hell, compared with the character you are playing?

Hopefully I am typical of the majority of people who see sex as being pretty close to the surface in every situation and I feel the needle on the dial of my personal 'sexometer' registering some degree of seismic activity in the different circumstances of each day; at work or at home, in the street or a foyer, a bar, a meeting, the supermarket, watching television or a ballet, with close friends or perfect strangers. As the needle flickers at the lowest readings or swings wildly at the top, there will be changes to the look in the eye, the play of the features, the behaviour, the rhythms of thinking and speaking, carriage and demeanour, in response to the energy flows within. The real who-you-are is very much a matter of what, in sex, you enjoy or fantasise about, what you crave or seek to avoid, what responsibilities you accept and powers you assert or yield to. Just as in sex itself you will incline towards dominance, flexibility, timidity or recklessness, masochism or sadism, so your body will reflect many other aspects of your life. How you shrink from it or indulge in this great celebration of being alive, how you reveal it or hide it, is an indication of your own, and your character's individuality.

Spiritual Energy

The presence or absence of spiritual energy is the key to a particular character. It is perhaps best to define 'spiritual' in terms of relating to the soul, to what is considered sacred and moral rather than material. The fires that fuel the spiritual dynamo are capable of producing a blinding light and spectacular heat. The graph line that represents the spiritual range will alert you to possibilities that range from a complacent sense of self-righteousness or a humble certainty, through all the intermediate gradations to blazing religious fanaticism and ecstasy.

Imaginative and creative energy

Two more categories of energy use that are worth considering for a richer analysis of character are imaginative energy and creative energy. There are people who are best explained in terms of these qualities. Using my graph to establish the full spectrum of dramatic possibilities it might range from the example of an artist so passionate about his creative work that nothing and no one could compete with it, to that of an individual so lacking in imaginative resources that he must find diversion in the world outside.

Qualities of Energy

Though the energy force itself is invisible, several of its manifestations can be clearly seen in the way it is being applied. In the sports you play, the skills you learn, and in your everyday activities, we will be able to distinguish at least six expressions of energy— sustained or lyrical, percussive, sudden or explosive, vibratory, suspended, collapsed and swinging—and two distinct categories of energy use, bound and free.

I have come to recognise the sustained and constantly-flowing release of energy as the dominant one in my movement makeup. 'Free' is more my natural state than 'bound'. Of these two, I use free to apply to movement that releases the energy created from its inner source—out through the muscle, the gesture, the limb, the release point, into the spaces beyond the body. Bound is a word I reserve for movement in which the energy is contained and held within the muscle in a way that denies its outward flow. Both are expressive and are present in all of us, often in the form of degrees of tension and relaxation.

Sustained and percussive

A sustained pattern of energy use produces movement that maintains a fairly constant dynamic, regardless of time or space use. Obvious examples are the behavioural, physical responses most of us make when present at official events, when participating in a public occasion at which we are a delegate, adjudicator, guest-of-honour or company representative—occasions that require at least the look of control and inner calm. There's no denying that in today's corporate and business-oriented societies, physical qualities become intellectual and temperamental symbols. A composed, energised exterior, an attentive focus, economical and precise gestures, a firm handshake, an aligned physicality that generates a smooth, easy, sustained flow of energy, will be read as indicators of quiet authority, self-discipline and sophistication, a focused mind, social ease, emotional stability and a tidy mind. Percussive energy is fired off, spark-like, to activate movement in sudden spurts and with clear-cut rhythms and dynamics. These fidgety, jerky, abrupt and explosive movements are more likely to be seen as symbolic of inner tension, instability, erratic concentration, doubtful leadership potential or authority. All of which may, or may not, be the case.

Vibratory

The use of 'vibratory' energy has something of both the percussive and sustained elements. The speed alone of the repetitive rhythms and dynamics of the movement produced make the form's characteristic quiverings, jigglings and drummings, a separate and distinct grouping. These are reactions to fairly extreme feelings and circumstances, and can be as hard to control and conceal in public situations as they are difficult to reproduce convincingly in staged ones. When experimenting with both vibratory movement and its accompanying feelings and transformations, it is important to remember the rapturous, and intensely pleasurable sources of the form as well as the fearful, cold and anxious situations that seem to be chiefly associated with it.

Suspension

What you see in a suspended movement is a temporary stop, a held pause, a moment of a movement sequence maintained in time. It could be a response to such promptings as a surprise or shock, either great or small, either pleasant or unpleasant; a need to allow time for the mind to settle on the next course of action, or the senses to interpret their environment. Though the moment is static, the energy, the dynamic inside the suspension, can be rich and pregnant with potential for the action that will follow. It can represent that most cherished phenomenon: the moment of change, when one idea is overtaken by another, when the body and mind are suddenly filled with a fresher realisation, when feelings intensify or reduce, when one energy quality takes over from another and when a change in the established atmosphere requires a new tactic and a change of action.

I know quite a few people, mainly women, for whom a suspended arm and hand position is their normal stance. They are seldom seen standing with their arms relaxed at their sides. More frequently the forearm is bent up and held at the elbow level, as though they were carrying a handbag and gloves. What gestures they perform maintain a floating quality and involve little else but the forearm and the hands and wrists. Questions and exclamations are frequently expressed in this suspended energy form, the question having its centre in the head, and the exclamation in the chest and the breath. All surprises have that instant of suspension, and are registered by the body

He would always talk about possibility, the suspended moment before someone moves and therefore the moment before someone speaks. It has been immensely helpful in film.
CATE BLANCHETT

with a lifted and backward reaction, whether the surprise is welcome or dreaded. The capacity to control suspended gesture and body action is a point of technique for public speakers, lecturers, storytellers, and comedians, to emphasise a word or idea, to tantalise an audience by making them wait for what is to come, to regain the fading attention of tiring listeners.

Just as 'suspend' fights against gravity, its opposite, 'collapse', yields to it. The shutdown of energy supply causes the body, whole or in part, to cave in, drop, fall in on itself and downwards towards the earth. The collapse can take a variety of forms. It can be a sudden, all-at-once drop of the entire body, or a limb or body part as tiny as a finger or an eyelid. The action may be a 'successive' one, that is, the 'collapse' may originate in a single centre and continue as a sequence of falling parts as the energy drains away from each unit in turn. Succession applies equally to movement built on unfolding and developing action that grows, wave-like, from a point of impulse in the body to eventually involve the whole organism. 'Collapse' need not be complete. The merest beginning of a collapse can be clearly evident in someone who feels faint, is overcome with fatigue, boredom or despair, or is in a state of depression. It can combine and alternate with other energy qualities, as in the staggering and reeling of a bad skater or someone in a wounded or drunken condition in which it appears uncertain whether 'collapse' or 'suspend' will win.

Swinging

Swinging combines the action of collapse-and-suspend with the dynamic of percussive-and-sustained. In a sequence of swings, strong energy initiates the phrase till the energy fades to a moment of suspension before gravity takes over in a rebound action. As a high-energy action it accompanies strong, even exalted moments of feeling.

It is a natural element when you walk and is closely connected to the soft, strong, 'collapse'-'suspend' act of breathing. The risings and fallings of this form can range from the most subtly sensuous and delicate to movement that suggests abandonment and surrender to heights and depths of hysteria, spiritual fervour or self-destruction.

Applying energy

The benefits that arise from explorations of these qualities include:

- building a checklist of qualities to use as reference points that can become part of a more thorough process of analysis than you might otherwise use;
- building your sense of identity, self-discovery and self-perception as you come to know your dominant and recessive energy qualities, thus determining the forms needing further experiment;
- analysing more precisely the dynamic make-up of the roles you study, and distinguishing them in specifically actorly terms from others you have played and from yourself;
- facilitating the search for the truthful, subtle and precise details of inner life and outer behaviour that will make specific the characterisation being sought.
- Adding to the ways that the complexity of human nature, complete with all its theatrically-interesting contradictions, idiosyncrasies and less apparent qualities, can be revealed in a context that helps solve the problems of characterisation.

Two particular applications of energy come to mind when discussing the importance of energy at work in us and the differing qualities of 'energy in action'. One is the need to hold on to the energy characteristics of your role and to resist merging them with the levels of energetic responses of your fellow actors. The second is the vital function of energy in realising the full potential of your entrances and exits.

Entrances, exits and maintaining your energy

There is a contagious disease rife among casts of actors. Unless they take precautions, they catch one another's speech rhythms, pitch ranges, body rhythms, speed and dynamics, and gravitate into each other's aura. As a consequence, they lose their own individuality. The symptoms are easily spotted: failing, on an entrance, to bring onto the scene energy specific to the moment and the character, energy that should provide a fresh dimension to the existing atmosphere on stage.

The treatment is not difficult. It is a matter of registering the voices and energies of each moment of the play's progression so that you can judge the levels and create contrasts—whether that means coming in over, or under, or in empathy with, the prevailing aura. In other words, not contrast for the sake of contrast but as a dramatic counterpoint in the unfolding texture of the action.

It is phenomenal how much information you can bring to your entrance onto stage, and how much an audience can read into the first two seconds of your arrival, well before any word is uttered. The arrival of a character of whom we know nothing, nor can we guess what bearing he or she might have on the succeeding action, is a big moment for that character, the actor and for us as audience. Each entrance should add an element, and an energy, that only that character can bring, because of who they are and how they express themselves. The new presence should show the changing contexts of intentions, circumstances, obstacles and motives that make up the substance of the play and the journey of that character through it. Gender, age and the significance of the individual's physicality register immediately—tall, fat, short, sloppy, heavy, well-groomed, over-dressed, untidy, tense, alert, slow, fast... a million possibilities. The posture and the body shape, the gestures and speed of entry, the focus and the energy levels—the audience receives information by the tonne. Similarly, a good actor does more than simply remove his presence when he exits. He takes with him those same elements of personal energy, and changes the atmosphere by taking the focus and interest with him, or leaving behind an aftertaste, a loss, making us aware of spaces and conditions of the offstage world, and settling or disturbing the onstage tensions and activities.

These are not just facts. They are data, evidence, the alphabet on which we base our readings of the language of theatre, the outward and visible signs of inner qualities that an audience needs to grasp, to interpret the play and the players. In life, one look at someone as they enter your space and you will know, or think you know, their state of health, the mood they are in, whether you wish to be with them or avoid them, whether you would employ them, trust them or where in your category of temperament you would place them. Something in that first look will make you warm to her, be turned off by him, impress, intrigue, or even repel you. In life, the power of that first impression can be so strong that it can take years to let it go. Many an actor has been chosen at audition on the strength of this.

A good actor's entrances and exits also supply the continuum of the onstage and offstage worlds, and can connect them in the mind of the audience through his thinking, believing, focus and body language to the extent that they are convinced of the reality of what they cannot see. Exits and entrances should have greater significance than just coming on stage or going off. There should always be a sense of 'destination'. In performance, they don't just come on or go off, but come from somewhere and return to somewhere.

As an actor you know the whole picture, and you may find yourself wanting to reveal the whole character on your first entrance. But it is much more exciting when you reveal facets of the role, quality by quality, scene by scene, entrance after entrance, in the same manner as the author makes us wait, page after page, so that the reader knows everything only at the last.

Of course, there are exceptions. I remember working on huge productions, like *Nicholas Nickleby* and *Peer Gynt*, in which the actors each played several roles, many of which were quite small. The task there was to bring on the full story of these characters in one immediately recognisable bundle, to say everything at once. Unfolding the rich complexities of a long and leading role, or encapsulating quickly the past and present, inner and outer qualities of a tiny cameo role, both require remarkable skills and sensitive preparation.

Weight

Physicists define weight as the force exerted on a mass by gravity. For too many of us weight can represent a limitation to our movement and carries only a negative connotation. Finding ways to turn weight into a mechanism of free and flowing movement rather than allowing it to be a burden should engage all your ingenuity.

Weight can be seen as a symbol of what you feel and want at any given moment. I believe strongly that acting is a matter of insightful differentiation. Your weight can lift and lighten with your loves and best hopes; it can sink within you, take you towards the floor and drag you down with boredom and despair; it can launch you into action of every kind, from violent to the most tender; it is shocked backwards into your body with every moment of surprise; it is that lump of lead in your guts in times of depression and disappointment and it is the wings that take you on your flights of ecstasy. It is something that can be released, directed, aimed, diverted, retracted, halted, accelerated, flung, floated, suspended. I watch it as a force in people's bodies, as a dynamo, a fuel for movement and as a barometer of their changing states of feeling.

Common usage includes many references to weight that confirm the fact that we all experience it in a variety of forms. People tell us of the weight of their responsibilities, the weight of troubles and cares; they describe the feeling of being weighed down with guilt and regret, with expectation, envy or tragedy. Writers express certain events as lifting a weight off our minds. Directors ask their casts to give more weight to the roles or to lighten the quality of their characterisation. Throughout the ageing process I have felt my weight—that is, my body's heaviness—to be at war with my cherished mobility and my former capacity for speed, flow and agility. If I am not watchful, it is my legs that take me for a walk rather than me setting my body weight in motion and making my legs remain my servants. As is the case with much of the study of Movement, weight is a feeling as well as a metaphor. And it needs to be felt and acknowledged in a kinaesthetic and sensory way if, as artists, we are to manipulate and experiment with it technically.

One of my own responses to the sensation and awareness of weight within me has produced an image that can be effective. I sense it as a kind of core, substantial but volatile, fluid, even potentially turbulent, a bit like my personal concept of the earth's molten core, full of the potential to flow, expand, erupt, subside and settle, swirl, or build up

Keith Bain, studio shot 1974.

pressure and move off in any direction, taking me with it. I can feel it respond to any tilt or shock, whether caused by me or exerted on me by some outside force. Of all the substances of which this core might be composed, mercury produces the most graphic example. Hold a drop of mercury, still, in your hand. Its potential to adjust to the slightest of impulses is not only apparent but can be felt, viscerally. The mercury inside me has the added capacity to be activated by my mental and emotional states, to be my thoughts and desires in action. The particularity of the thought creates the particularity of my core's response. I can feel that weight inside me retract and retreat in the presence of anything I wish to avoid. It is a comfortable inner strength and a great support when I am in familiar and unthreatening company. I feel it magnetised and poised to move out to whatever catches my interest. It tugs at me and pulls me from position to position in space in accordance with my whims and wishes. It is high and tight in my chest one moment and down in my boots at another. I can feel it drag behind me when I must do what I least want to do or go where I don't want to go. In moments of urgency I feel it released out of myself into the space ahead of me and I am drawn along in its wake.

Dynamics

Dynamics can be equated with release of energy, and can be considered in terms of a scale. The lower end of the scale being leaden, lethargic with little energy output, and the upper literally bursting with energy, an almost manic state. In the centre is a neutral state where energy is at a point of equilibrium. There are so many changes through this scale that if you fully explore each point along it you will learn how to shift and change your energy appropriately for any given moment in a scene. You also become aware of where your own personal energy sits, what you are most comfortable with and how to understand and control your energy. This dynamic range allows you to complement and react to each other's energy. You should also be aware when energy is flagging, or others are picking up on the same energy as you. This can lead to a dull monotone performance. It is the dynamic differences between us that spark the drama; it is this exchange of energy that sometimes contains more information than the text.

In assessing your dynamic range, look for the ability:

• to access easily all states of energy;
• to be capable of total physical engagement with that energy;
• to fully express and embody that energy;
• to be able to adjust your energy appropriately—to 'turn up/down the volume knobs'. To change the atmosphere of a scene; you need to focus your energy strongly enough to affect others in the scene as well as the audience.

EXERCISE IN ENERGY AWARENESS AND DYNAMIC RANGE

Locate the source of each particular type of energy, where it manifests in your body, the level of energy and to what extent it is released or withheld. The combination of these uses of energy should produce a dynamic, articulated and clear performance. Experiment with increasing and decreasing the varying energy levels in a range of various activities. It is important that you also learn to extend your dynamic range beyond the everyday so that you can inhabit convincingly characters who are in extreme situations and therefore in extreme states.

JULIA COTTON

6

Characterisation

You have to be able to pick up your character and transport it to different places—character-work is so wonderful like that. I remember Keith saying, as you're walking around as your character, things like, 'You are late for the funeral of your best friend. The only seat left is right at the front and you have to walk down to the front with everybody looking at and speaking about you.' Then you might go into a neutral state before returning to your character. This time Keith would say, 'Now your character is going to receive an award from the Queen,' or maybe, 'You are walking down the street and you see a $5 note.' As an actor you have all these wonderful choices; do you pick it up and ask other people if it is theirs; or do you slip it in your pocket; or do you ignore it completely? In film work this is fantastic because you can go anywhere with your character. The director can throw any changes at you and it's not a problem, just an opportunity to do something different. It really puts you in the moment with all the possibilities.

SONIA TODD

Here's a big one, if not *the* big one.

Characterisation is where so much of all the acting theory, the voice and speech work, the Movement training, the improvisations and skills should be leading, and where they all meet.

When we talk of characterisation we are talking creativity, and when creativity enters the discussion, we are dealing with complex elements such as inspiration, talent, intuition, instinct, insight, judgment and imagination. Characterisation is not a single or simple process, having several stages of intellectual, psychological, imaginative, instinctive, technical and physical considerations to be dealt with. Troubles can arise at any one of these stages.

The intellectual stage

The intellectual stage addresses the crucial need to understand the task ahead. So many of your less-than-successful ventures are likely to be the result of the failure to have analysed, realised or understood sufficiently deeply the circumstances of your endeavours. In drama, if you don't deeply understand what lies inside and behind the text, or the instruction, situation, theme or whatever the original source material happens to be, then you will be structuring your work on faulty foundations.

There are things to understand. Apart from the obvious ones surrounding the question of who this new character is, in all its richness and complexity, you need to understand who everyone else is, what drives them and how their motives and personalities connect or clash with your own. You need to understand the twists and turns of the plot lines and the implications arising from the theme. You need to understand the structure and the rhythm of the whole piece, to interpret the world in which the characters function, to appreciate the reason-for-being of all the characters in the play, to know the true nature of their differing relationships, as well as the obstacles that lie in their way.

If your understanding of these is imperfect, the discoveries of the imagination will be similarly defective. As a result, the inner life of the character will be enlivened by ill-suited images, the psychology of the role impaired and the resulting physical responses will be inappropriate and out-of-character. Expressed in another way the more intimate and complete the understanding, the more likelihood there will be for attaining the harmony between the body and psychology, and for your body to be moulded and recreated from the inside.

More often than not, it is the depth or the shallowness of the understanding, rather than a misunderstanding, that makes the difference. It is pretty obvious that characterisation based on a peripheral, facile and self-concerned understanding would produce results that reflect these limiting qualities. The most positive and courageous work will develop out of understanding that has the greatest certainty, conviction and depth. Others have published systems for analysing texts and researching background material. For my part, I encourage you to pursue a systematic approach to understanding that reveals the heart of the piece and the protagonists, and in doing so, touches your heart.

Of special importance is the understanding not only of the positive qualities of your character, but of the predicaments, the contradictions, the inconsistencies, the flaws and imperfections. I would advise you to come to terms with these deeper-hued characteristics early in the research period, accepting them without qualification. After all, these attributes are typical of every one of us and are the truest marks of our common humanity.

It is not always the actor with the highest IQ who is praised for the clear intelligence underlying his characterisation. The truly creative artist has the ability to transform the information they receive into thrillingly artistic visualisations. Similarly, I could name actors with a gift of natural talent that allows them to bypass a lot of the intellectual preparation and instead trust to instinct, impulse and the accident of inspiration. I know others who faithfully follow, step by step, one of the common acting theories. Some make their discoveries through play, testing the limits of physical and dramatic possibilities as in children's games.

Anything that succeeds in increasing knowledge and understanding can only be a good thing.

A fully considered process leads many actors to their proudest characterisations. Not only will the text be scrutinised for every detail of the character's inner and outer life, but vital statistics, a life history and facts never considered by the author will be invented to allow the actor to know the role in the most complete and intimate way. Stories abound of actors whose research includes living for a time in actual condi-

'I never inhaled.' Studio shot, Temora 1952

tions, such as prisons, work places, asylums, monasteries, factories, brothels, squats and so on—so that in the play or film they are not guessing at the character's situation but reliving it as authentically as possible.

My preference is for a balance of what can be acquired and analysed, and what arises from imagination, impulse and spontaneity. Characterisations that are planned in their every detail, controlled from the head, fixed in form against modification and variation, and unsympathetic to the range of atmospheres and accidents which are part of most performances, chill me to the bone. But, whether understanding comes easily and naturally, or is the consequence of close study and scrupulous method, it is basic to the other procedures that follow.

The imaginative and psychological stages

Information and understanding start the characterisation cycle. The imagination will continue this work for you, until you are so well-informed, and so acutely identified with this new human being, that you begin to see with that person's eyes, think with their brain, speak with their voice and share their psychology.

The term 'psychology' in the jargon of acting practice refers more to the mental characteristics and attitudes of a person or group, and to the mental factors governing a situation or activity, than to the idea of a scientific study of the human mind in action. I make this point because I consider it unhelpful for actors to function as if they were clinical psychologists. Most of us have trouble enough coming to terms with our own psychology. You face the even more difficult task of intimately understanding the inner working of another character's mind; to think and react as they do and experience appetites and attitudes as if they are your own. A person's psychology will determine their behaviour and movement qualities. But more vital and dramatically valid are the motivational forces within their psychological workings. These can't be directly seen but nevertheless must be revealed through the physicality of the performer—to reveal not just what they do but why they do it.

Motivation and justification are golden words for any performing artist and are the links between thought and action. The actor trained in the techniques of action-objective work, as propounded by Stanislavski, creates and maintains that link, ensuring credibility and truth in performance. The relevance of accurate understanding to this degree of identification with another's psychology is, I hope, obvious.

The instinctive stage

Now let's look at the instinctive ingredients of the characterisation process. All the inborn qualities of imagination, intuition, insight, inspiration, instinct and talent are not easily or consciously controlled or dependent on particular stimuli. For our purposes, the best definitions of such properties could be unconscious skill, inborn creative force, sudden brilliant idea, spontaneous knowing without reasoning, creative mental faculties able to form images and concepts about non-present things—and all of them opposing the notion of being learned, calculated, or premeditated. As for talent, I like to describe it as the inherent capacity to do easily what other people find difficult. I recommend the works of people like Uta Hagen for explicit discussion of cognitive techniques such as personalisation, particularisation, endowment, sensory stimuli, emotional and sensory memory, physical and mental animation, sense of destination, transference and action-objective work.*

To summarise—the evidence for both the outer details and the inner landscape of each role you will play lies in the script. Your intellectual understanding of the textual treasure of the piece leads towards a psychological understanding of the role. This, together with your imaginative and instinctual processes, generates the movement and behaviour that, in turn, serve the audience as evidence of the playwright's and the actor's intentions. Sounds simple, doesn't it? Maybe not, but it is pretty logical.

Technical and physical considerations

Theorists and renowned performers will continue to add new techniques to those already practised to deepen the inner preparation for character creation. But what is the good of all this knowing, all this information and psychological priming if your body is technically deficient? What is the point of having a body that cannot expressively and technically respond to the images and ideas that your brain and imagination are capable of dreaming up? What if your artistic visualisations are beyond your physical capacity to realise? What if your mannerisms and dynamic range are so restrictive that no matter how distinctly you conceive your characters they all come out the same, and suspiciously similar to yourself?

---

*   Uta Hagen (1919–2004), eminent Broadway actress and teacher, was the author of several best-selling acting texts.

Paula Arundell and Duncan Young in *Ghetto*: Dir. Ros Horin, NIDA 1995.

Paula Arundell and Peter Kowitz in *Blackbird*: Dir. Cate Blanchett, Sydney Theatre Company 2007.

One of the most difficult of all the physical techniques, harder perhaps than the elaborate skills of gymnastics, mime and dance, is the technique of telling the truth through the body, of communicating the most delicate refinement of thought and feeling, with simplicity, economy, pleasure and ease. If these are relevant questions, then perhaps the reverse is worth asking—what is the point of having a body trained to accomplish unbelievable physical and technical feats that can't deal with the expression of ideas and feelings?

Another question immediately arises. What use can be made of the knowledge accumulated about the character to be played and the play to be performed if it is not balanced by accurate self-knowledge? What hope have you got if you are mistaken about your nature, your degree of vulnerability, your physical and temperamental makeup or the effect you have on others, when you are required to create another character out of this inaccurately perceived self? Differentiating between yourself and the character would be problematic, to say the least. Recognising and identifying your own feelings and true nature can only make it easier to recognise those of an assigned character. So, looking into and exploring yourself is a good starting point for the next task of characterisation let alone the rest of your career.

Self-perception

In this search for self-perception I find that we go one of two ways. There are those of us who give ourselves credit for a vastly more spectacular list of admirable and beguiling qualities than of negative ones. If you are one of these people, you might fail to consider how your thoughts and actions might be spiteful, vindictive and deceitful. That you are, in fact, capable of making stupid decisions, behaving dangerously or cruelly; of wishing ill of other people, of making unfair judgments and pitiless or ungenerous statements, of lying, jealousy, even murder. But if you can face the fact that in certain circumstances you have proved to be as gauche and tactless, arrogant, devious and high-handed, as prejudiced and immodest as any character in literature, then you have a chance of dealing honestly and un-judgmentally with whatever roles you are privileged to play.

If however, you are super-sensitive, you may have confronted your episodic experiences of cowardliness, quick temper, phobias, snobbery and indecisiveness, but have not looked inside deeply enough for evidence of your warmth, ease and enthusiasm, your capacity for imperiousness and confrontational strength. This is where the value of Movement comes in. Owning your own body and pursuing an intimate knowledge of yourself, getting out of your own way, getting past the blocked sensations of a tense, tentative and wooden body, developing a thinking, feeling and speaking body, responsive and available to the moment, versatile and uninhibited, is what studying Movement is meant to achieve. So that, when you need it, you have a body that serves you both in roles that are close to you and so far away the transformation is absolute.

I have declared my belief in the body's ability to provoke or recreate emotional and psychological states through action and gesture, as well as the other way round. It is absolutely possible to work backwards from the effect to the cause. For instance, you don't have to thump a table-top with a clenched fist more than a couple of times before feeling your whole being flood with rising anger or aggression. Not only will the emotional state be created but your mindset will correspondingly be changed as if the real circumstances were the cause. Not everyone has this gift to the same degree, but it can be exercised and made more sensitive with practice.

EXERCISE IN RECREATING EMOTIONAL AND PSYCHOLOGICAL STATES

Choose a single sentence from a script and allow yourself, each time you repeat that sentence, to open up to the impulses that result from a series of physical adjustments. Even the simplest adjustments—things like changes of weight and body angle, degrees of stillness and activity, a variety of body gestures, fresh points of focus, changes of distance, speeds and energies, changes of dynamics, the finger you choose to point with—can produce results that are a reminder of how new life can be breathed into stale phrasings, emphases and meanings when the body and the mind work in empathetic unison. It can be of help at those times in rehearsal when inspiration fails and a block in the creative process of characterisation holds back progress.

Starting points

It fascinates me to learn from how many different starting points our best actors proceed. Some work from the inside out and some prefer from outside in. Some like to begin boldly, almost excessively, and gradually,

Keith would encourage us to explore the details that could be the character's physicality. He would talk about their fingers and what point they would lead from physically. Reflected back to you in the mirrors in the classroom. He was very interested in you having an objective and subjective sense of who you were and what you were doing.

CATE BLANCHETT

during early rehearsals, pare away the bigness of their gesture and sound till they find the most refined way to say what the author has indicated. We have all heard of other actors whose first rehearsals are so underplayed, that the director and the cast become concerned about when and in which direction that actor might eventually take off. In a few famous cases, it has taken the entire rehearsal period before anyone has seen what the final product might be. This might work well for the person concerned but is pretty tough on those players whose approach depends on adapting to, and being influenced by, their fellow actors.

It is common for productions to devote the first week or so to sitting around the table in deep discussion about every aspect of the play. This is ideal for anyone who builds their performance on analysis and concept but can be frustrating for someone for whom play, action and interaction is the favoured process. And it is possible to 'talk about' the play for days and then find, in the first few moments of moving into the space, that something altogether fresh happens and that there are other and better ways to play the scenes.

'Fleshing out' a character

Some of the most commonly heard notes given by directors to floundering cast members are to do with 'fleshing out' their characters, finding detail that will add dimension and specificity to characters that are remaining general, colourless and ambiguous. The wide eyes and stunned expressions I see in response to directors' notes like these make it clear that 'detailing' is for many a mysterious concept.

A detail is a small but telling item of activity which is so pertinent that it defines an essential element of motive or temperament and pinpoints the truth of a character and moment. It is more than an embellishment, it can be as subtle as the lowering of the eyelids or the considered way a prop is used. It could be the well-judged timing of a line or move.

Just as the request to an actor for an increase in energy is often answered by his speaking louder and moving faster, so the plea for richer detail can result in unjustifiable behaviour, unproductive gestures, and distracting movement. In other words, activity for its own sake. This takes the audience no deeper into the character's life, doing more but saying less. Few actors in such a situation consider that doing less, not more—even doing nothing, just being attentively still— could be the preferred way to bring significant detail to a scene and a character.

One example was rehearsing a group of actors playing young North-Country English working girls of the same age, same background, education and situation. The problem became one of finding details that would differentiate the characters who had so many qualities in common. In a scene where two of them are preparing for another big night out, checking their make-up in the one mirror, one of them was able to reveal a greater thoughtfulness and softer nature by offering her lipstick to the other just before using it herself. The brusque rejection of this gesture by the second girl with a quick, hard look, a slight shrug and a pull of the mouth, established the temperamental contrast. This interchange was achieved in no more than a second or two. It wasn't ornamental or a distracting bit of business. And its statement was complete and said as much about the relationship and their status in the group as it did about their individual attributes. Each actress was helped by the other to make statements that would have been difficult to express alone.

EXERCISE TO EXPLORE DETAIL IN CHARACTERISATION

This exercise involves starting with a neutral walk, then making some small adjustment such as turning the toes in slightly, or out, walking more on the outside or inside of the foot, taking longer or shorter than normal strides. Keith would work through the body in this way—arms swinging more than usual, or perhaps rounding the shoulders; different angles of the head; and eyes with different focus points. In between each adjustment the students would return to a neutral walk to better understand and to experience the changes of thought, mood, emotion, outlook, energy and tempo brought about by the smallest degree of physical adjustment. Keith would ask them with each adjustment, 'How does the world look to you now?' or, 'How do you feel about other people?' 'Where in the room do you feel most comfortable?' Having explored many variations and possibilities, the students could then identify and select those adjustments that suited their character, that felt 'right'. This way the student had the opportunity to try things out to find the right 'fit' and most importantly they were able to discover and then make choices about the character's physicality themselves. They could also begin to understand the amount of detail they could work with and how changing their physicality even minimally gave them limitless possibilities to explore.

JULIA COTTON

Literalness

Guard against too literal a response to the representation of character and their inner-outer life. Literal is not a bad starting point, but that is only where the search begins.

Particular occupations and intensive training programs often leave an indelible imprint on the body that registers as a kind of mannerism or gesture. The turned-out legs, the lengthened spine, the poised head, long neck and placed body of the dancer are scars that many will carry to the grave. A professional soldier, a fashion model, a top executive, an outdoor labourer, a weight lifter and a body builder are just a few examples of folk who have modified their original mannerisms to the point of replacing old habits with new ones.

A warning here: while a study of these aspects of characterisation can lead you to interesting detail, it can also encourage that kind of indicative acting that consists of labelling every moment and characteristic, and represents the playing of your researches rather than the actual text. I am reminded of an eager actor, so diligent in the background studies of a play, who, when cast as a young officer in a Chekhov work, presented him as if he were on permanent sentry duty, even though the scene was set in the drawing room of a country estate. Suggestions, whiffs, glimpses and mere flavours of qualities are often preferable, and sufficient to be revealing. Contradictions and exceptions can be more truthful and dramatically effective than the obvious, and playing against it frequently strengthens the impact.

Every attribute you ascribe to a role is as dangerous as it is useful. Every adjective you use to distinguish this character can lead you in directions it was never intended to go or could hold you fixed to the spot. Rather than limiting the character to a literal 'proudness' for instance, search to discover the degree and range of his pride. Under what circumstances does this quality flourish or subside? At what points in the play is it most clearly manifested? Is he proud of his pride, ashamed of it, or even conscious of it? What does it make him do, what details of behaviour will result from it? What kind of pride is it? Is it a high-and-mighty arrogance, is it smug and egotistical, or is it a vanity and an overvaluing of himself? Or, for instance, is it the proper pride of a parent for their child's achievements? To what degree does your character suppress it, if at all? Some of the great dramatic moments for us as audience are when we see a proud man's pride bruised, destroyed or lost.

A further application of literalness comes in the playing of emotional states. One of the drama teacher's hardest tasks is to wean students away from the idea of identifying scenes and sections of the play as the sad bit, the angry bit, the jealous bit, and then playing those emotional states without considering them as the outcome of a character's objectives, or a response to his circumstances. Playing, displaying, indulging in emotion is a great turn-on for actors. It must be, because so many of them do it. What is worse, it leads them to the most blatant and unsubtle demonstration of these generalised emotions. You can see them pumping and squeezing their feelings up from somewhere inside and manifesting all this in its most literal and predictable form—screaming and yelling on a relentless note for anger, head and upper body thrust forward and up close to their adversary, fists clenched and tension from top to toe. With this mindset, you are likely to play all angry scenes and angry characters in the same insensitive way and will be in no state to read your protagonist, adjust to their reaction or consider the possibilities of finding control instead of losing it, of increasing intensity by underplaying or playing against the emotion.

You must do what is natural to the character. You need to present the complete character and allow the rest of the world to come to its own decisions. A judgmental state succeeds mostly in inhibiting creativity, making a parade of qualities expressed as your opinion about the character and not as a revelation of the character's motivations.

The reactive approach

Actors seldom take enough advantage of the support system surrounding them. It is often the case that an actor's preparation for a role involves such various and thorough investigations of the text, such deep searches within himself and such complicated technical and theoretical applications that it can isolate him from a lot of the support coming from the ensemble. Each actor's part is so precious it can engross the performer to the extent that it becomes more important than the whole piece itself. His concentration on the role can make him overlook the fact that several of the other characters discuss and describe him, treat him in specific ways and attribute to him status, quality, function and personality through their dialogue and their behaviour in his presence.

In a company of good performers, you are far from being alone in the portrayal of your role. Each actor in the cast is being endowed with characteristics and identity by every other actor. If the players are as assiduous in their partner's transformation into their character as they are for their own, then they will each have helped solve the other's problems and have lifted the full responsibility for the scene from their own shoulders. It creates an interdependence, even while playing an action on someone else.*

The idea of acting as 'reacting' ensures being in the moment and offers the best chance for spontaneity and the impulses that can arise in reactive situations. Your movement and behaviour are more likely to be honest and less self-aware when working in reaction to immediate circumstances than when it is imposed on the scene as a result of an earlier decision—made last night at home under the shower.

It's a question of finding a physically centered posture which becomes my habitual starting point. Then I put parts of my body 'off centre' (head forward, arms turned out, hips back, or whatever) and see what that suggests about the character's emotional world. By experimenting with various combinations I can usually come up with a physical representation which helps communicate the emotional, vocational and spiritual experience of the character. The fun part comes in choosing physical postures and gestures which betray the true nature of the character despite his protestations to the contrary.

JOHN HOWARD

Rehearsals are designed for experimenting with infinite possibilities, not just finding things that seem to work. All the elements that Movement consists of—what you do and how you do it, your body use and your response to space, time and energy, your gestures, your mannerisms and behaviour—are worth experimenting with so that none of the qualities that make your character special are overlooked

---

* Playing an action: According to Laban theory every gesture, stage action, line—everything you do on stage—needs to affect someone. There are psychological and physical 'actions'. These are characterised by verbs—so with the line, 'You didn't come over last night' the reason for the line could be 'to lecture' or 'to remind' (psychological action). How you actually say the line, for example 'to needle' or 'to slap', is the physical action.

in the process. They make up a long checklist, I know, but subtlety, truth, dimension and artistry are the wonderful rewards.

It is worth repeating: you will seldom need to invent every quality that a character possesses. So be content to play the differences between you. There will surely be some common features —physical, age-wise, temperamental, intellectual—that you share to a degree and free you of the need to labour your imagination. It will be rare indeed to be given a role that demands that you suppress every one of your own qualities and construct a fresh creation altogether.

As we have seen, there are many points of reference to check when creating a character. But ideally, the more roles you play the less self-conscious and the more ingrained these references should become. Characters need deepening, not decorating. They thrive on enrichment, not elaboration. It is essence that counts, and the journey is to get as close as possible to that essence. Once that has been identified, you will know what you must believe, and then you must believe it to the degree that will convince everyone who witnesses it.

7

Gesture

He taught me that you don't have to do big
gestures everywhere when there are twenty or
forty of you on stage. The smaller the better.

BRIAN CROSSLEY

I am always wary when it comes to discussions about gesture, chiefly because you might get the impression that gestures and gesturing are a strictly codified practice; that there are hard-and-fast rules to be followed. There were times when actors conveyed their inner states and much of the storyline by standardised rhetorical gestures representing 'the passions'. These gestures were instantly recognised by the audiences of the period. The convention of the acting I first encountered in the mid-1940s was one of placed and planned body gestures, illustrated reactions and simulated emotional responses. At rehearsal all the groupings, the stage picture and the movement details were fixed, written down in each actor's script and the stage manager's copy, never to be tampered with for the length of the run. Compared with today this approach was 'external', concerned primarily with form and style. To be described as stylish was praise indeed.

Before the 1960s, a would-be actor began his career in an informal way, 'on the hoof' you might say, watching and copying his favourites in action, noting the way they sat, stood, and smoked a cigarette, imitating their inflections, their tricks of timing, gestures and mannerisms. After a successful audition for a small role the copying and borrowing no doubt increased, and like any other apprentice, the up-and-coming thespian took on whatever seemed to work well for his idols. In short, the actor learned by imitation and by the act of rehearsing and performing. Little of what they did onstage arose from a concern for truthful behaviour or was supported by a personal method of theoretical and psychological research that incorporated impulse and spontaneity into their performance.

There is no place in the actor training systems of today for those codified gestural procedures—like ascribing to the familiar gesture of crossing the arms in front of the chest the meaning of a barrier, a warning or confrontation. Such a gesture may well indicate that intention but only in a certain range of contexts. Change the context and that same gesture could be sexually provocative, coy, or comfortably casual.

Gestures play such a huge part in our lives that they must play as big a role in our acting. We never stop making and modifying our gesture patterns. We are recognisable to others by the movements of all our body parts and by the range of flavours and energies in these gestures as we express and emphasise ideas, emotions and intentions. The surprise is that we move so much. We are seldom still. The body gestures range from the random, flailing and diffuse activity of a baby, to the uncertain moves of the elderly. They constitute a great part of what we call our mannerisms, and every actor needs to be alert to how repetitive and restricting these can become.

Using gestures well can become the most coherent aspect of your expressive equipment. Whenever words are impossible, gestures can do your speaking for you. The multitudinous movements of the body are a set of signals for sending messages. Take away your gestures and you would be hard to read, difficult to understand and reduced in your capacity to communicate. At worst our gestures are inhibited, self-conscious, inexplicit, borrowed, manufactured, ambiguous or dishonest. At best, they arise from the impulses and energies of our thinking, sensing, feeling, our nature and nurture. They come and go, hundreds of them in an hour, and all of them embodying something of our essence.

Many of your gestures will become habits. In certain circumstances they have that careful, controlled look, as if you have consciously and intellectually chosen them. Others have a born-of-the-moment spontaneity as though they have chosen themselves; some, are intended to deceive.

The tendency is to think that gestures are a matter of all the busy activity of your hands and arms, but that is a limited view. The body as a whole can make a gesture, as in a bow, a curtsy or a hug. The language of the head droops, tilts, nods and shakes. There are all the messages that eyebrows and forehead are forever sending; the stares and averted gazes, the widening and narrowing, the lowering and raising. Much of the focusing and defocusing of the eyes have the nature of gestures. In fact, the looks and glances that your eyes are capable of transmitting and receiving often have the gestural quality of touches and strokings, piercings and pressings. We all know about the looks that are hot or cold, and the looks that can kill. We regularly express looks that invite, reject, deny, warn, plead, question, desire, conspire, threaten and amuse, and that are no less powerful and no more ambiguous than the boldest of our physical actions.

I would also include as gestures the pattern of signals that your eyelids make, when their blinking and fluttering signify many more things than bodily necessity. The wrinkling of the nose can be a gesture of distaste or disapproval, and a mouth and jaw gesture one that reveals an unbelievable range of feelings.

Displacements of ribs and shoulders are among the most telling of the body's gesturing; and as for the legs and feet, I can never understand why these wonderfully explicit and descriptive regions are so often overlooked and under-exploited in the process of characterisation. They are as versatile and expressive as any body part; I can't think of an emotional or psychological state that cannot be indicated by some gestural adjustment of the lower limbs. Perhaps they turn in or out. There are shifts and changes of weight, a locking or bending of knees, shuffling, bouncing, scraping, shaking, fidgeting, crossing and uncrossing, twisting. They can show states of embarrassment, sophistication, guilt, boredom and lust as clearly as they can distinguish social class, status, historic period, occupation, age and temperament. Legs can be so funny, so sexy, so witty and they can be used to dramatic effect by giving evidence of the real feelings of a character as opposed to the pretences the upper body is conveying. The rhythmic possibilities of these neglected lower limbs, too, add to their articulation.

In general, actors when performing are inclined to use far too many gestures—many that add not a jot of clarity or specificity to the performance. It is obviously difficult for those actors to leave themselves alone. We take our gestures so much for granted that it can be quite salutary to analyse our usage and range. It would also be good to observe the gesture patterns of others, to note the effects on gestures of age, emotion, circumstance and ethnicity, and to appreciate the different families of gesture that can be distinguished. To help you in as many ways as possible, it is worth considering the range of human gesture from several different points of view. They can be analysed both from their outward and visible effect and their inward invisible cause; from the purposes they serve and the meanings they communicate; from their motivations and their dynamics; from their interaction with space, time and energy; from the degree to which they are explicit and direct, or implicit and promising.

If you watch someone recounting a story or an experience to a group of listeners, you are certain to recognise that the gestures serve different purposes, that they arise from different impulses and emotional centres, and achieve quite different results. The storyteller might begin with a set of gestures, probably wide, open-bodied and emphatic enough to catch everyone's attention and make him the centre of focus so that the story can begin. The gestures that then follow will be modified and flavoured by the teller's attitude and intention. If he wishes to make his audience laugh, thrill or share his amazement, his movements will doubtless be more buoyant and extrovert than if he is seeking sympathy or disgust. One set of gestures will emphasise, with a direct and energetic outgoing action, moments in the narrative the storyteller hopes will help the listeners absorb the situation and set up the atmosphere. There will be several body, eye and head turns as the speaker distributes the story among the listeners.

The next set may include a tilt of the head, a suspended arm gesture and an upward but inward-focused turn of the eye as the narrator tries to get his facts straight, searches in his mind for the precise word and turn of phrase, and reminds himself of important details by revisiting in his head the scene he is describing. This group of gestures is evidence of his remembering, and helps the storyteller with his own thinking rather than assisting the audience to follow the narrative.

There could follow a series of gestures that mime the actions being recounted—knocking on the door, getting money from his pockets, paying the driver, representing the explosion, running up the stairs, imitating several of the characters in the tale by taking on their shapes and mannerisms. Depending on his feelings about them, he may exaggerate, distort, even stylise, these qualities; idealise them, or try to represent as authentic a picture of them as he can. As the story brings back emotional memories, he could now reproduce gestures that take very much the same form as occurred in the original event, and that express again the same intensity of feeling as was experienced in the first place.

All of this might have been accompanied by repetitive gestures that are characteristic of the storyteller. Old, comfortable gestures like tapping or interlocking his fingers, hooking some hair behind his ear, holding one hand in the other, accenting key words with the flicks and dabs that have now become a habit. Doubtless, the need to offer the story to everyone in the group will produce another set of body gestures. And the quality of the movements, the energy behind them, their range and dynamic colouring will have been the product of the narrator's intention. The gestures could be fairly consistent with each retelling of the story, but if required to amuse or to impress, to appal or to warn, each of the gestures would have been differently expressed.

So diverse are the body responses to emotion, and to degrees of feeling, that it is possible to consider gestures on the basis of the emotional sources, the individual's intentions, or the impulses that rise from these, as well as the empathic relationship of the actor to his role. However, it could also be profitable to consider the outward forms that gestures of any category take. They could be categorised on the basis of their scope and range, their time values and their dynamic qualities. For instance, there could well be as many hand and arm gestures that involve touching, clutching, holding and enfolding your own body as there are ones that move out into the space around you. Here it is as valuable to analyse the body parts that are touched and held as it is to consider the pressures and the tensions of the gestures, as well as such details as which finger or part of the hand does the touching. Try making a gesture on some part of your face with each finger in turn: your fingertips, your fist, the back of your hand or the whole palm, and feel the different stories and scenarios that each one produces.

The following are categories into which most of our gestures fit.

Functional gestures

These are the ones that aim to achieve a practical purpose. They are infinite in number, and include examples like flicking through the leaves of a book, scratching an itch, rubbing a sore knee, picking some fluff off someone's jacket, wiping something nasty off your shoe, pointing out a specific object or direction, catching a moth, throwing a ball, wiping a tear, tossing the hair out of your eyes. But don't be fooled by all these practical-seeming activities. They are only truly functional if they are genuinely what they seem. You can scratch away at a part of you that is not in the least bit itchy. You look at your watch without needing to, not even registering the time. You may fix hair that didn't need tidying and smooth out clothes that hadn't a wrinkle in them. In these cases you are using what appear to be a productive functional gesture but which more likely serves a need to disguise an emotional state: to use up an excess of nervous energy or to hide your boredom, worry, impatience or self-consciousness. They seldom fool anyone and are great examples of the contradictions and ambivalence present in much human behaviour.

Sometimes, too, what starts out to be truly functional can be symptomatic of some strong emotion when the gesture is repeated, like the persistent straightening of a tie, checking make-up or looking through notes when facing a challenging event such as an interview, an audition or a speech.

Emotional gestures

These are the body's responses to emotional states. Not only do they vary from person to person and from situation to situation, but any one of us will have variations with which to express a similar state of feeling. How your body has expressed the same sorts of feelings but at different stages of your life, how you have modified your uninhibited gesturing as a child to conform with the changing self-images you pass through, how effectively your gestures serve these images of yourself, and how much you are betrayed by them, are investigations that could provide some interesting answers. This group includes the obvious ones of hugging, kissing, shaking a fist and the range of responses to exclamations and surprises, pleasant and unpleasant. Extreme emotional states are responsible for some of the most contorted body shapings, as well as the wildest rocking and shaking gestural patterns.

The gestures that rise from emotional states are even more eloquent, certainly more dramatic, when you observe the body's contrary promptings to control the pressure of feeling that is mounting inside. These emotions can emanate from the deepest centres; and it is usually the most vulnerable and guarded areas of the body that are most visibly affected—the throat, the open palms, the heart and the pelvic regions.

Few societies allow their citizens the luxury of full and unconditional expression of their real feelings. The general rule is to somehow balance the need to let our feelings out and the need to cover them up for social or cultural reasons. Consequently we are adept at monitoring and manipulating our gestures to cope with the situations that confront us every moment of the day. For instance, watch a young child at work in a supermarket manipulating his parents through his repertoire of body language to get what he wants and go where he wants. It seems worthwhile for you to remember that gestures are not all reflex actions, independent of the will, but can be consciously or unconsciously selected and performed.

It is difficult to find the best words to describe the small, fleeting, unfinished gestures which most of us use and which, if you counted them up, might well prove to outnumber all the overt, precise ones that people make. But I have settled on the expression 'nearly gestures'. I really love observing these at work in other people's behaviour and my own; their incompleteness is such an expressive statement of our inner uncertainties and insecurity.

Conventional gestures

These are gestures that have acquired an agreed significance, if not universally, then at least within particular cultures. They are movement codes, so accepted and recognisable that they can often be a substitute for, rather than an accompaniment to, speech. Most of them will have been taught to us by the example of adults before we reached the stage of using words. We are familiar with seeing parents encouraging the very young to nod their heads for a yes, shake their head for a no, wave goodbye or point to what it is they want. We have come to know that the wagging forefinger can be a warning, that raised eyebrows are asking a serious question, a frown can indicate doubt and disapproval and a shrug of the shoulders a rejection of responsibility. Nobody is in doubt when you beckon with your hands, arms and head that you want someone to come towards you; the spread and flexed hands at the end of long, straight arms is a clear indication to stop.

Then there is that range of indecent, belligerent and insulting gestures, normally involving one or more fingers energetically and vertically

Reg Livermore and Keith at rehearsals for Livermore's musical *Ned Kelly*: dir. Reg Livermore, chor. Keith Bain, Her Majesty's Theatre, Sydney 1978.

employed. We all recognise them, and use them from time to time. Of course, these same actions in different contexts can have a deeper and wider significance. The context, the timing and the dynamic quality of the gestures are what distinguish the one you want from the many other possible meanings.

Keith is one of the longstanding and more rewarding associations of my theatrical life. He adeptly sensed and explored the nub of my style by creating movement patterns within my capability that strengthened the dramatic or comedic intentions expected of me.

REG LIVERMORE

Emphatic gestures

The rhythms and stresses of all your thoughts and speech can be represented with gestures that seem to serve no other purpose than to underline the moments of emphasis. Even an apparently impartial presenter or newsreader on television can be seen to nod their head and upper body in time with their reading; and if they do achieve a neutral stillness they may still be seen to gesture the commas and the full stops, and especially the exclamations and question marks. The most distracting of their facial gestures are the busy eyebrows as the speaker tries to emphasise and animate the text.

These emphatic gestures not only give vigour, force and intensity to the main points expressed but double their meaning and intention by pointing up the degree of significance being applied by the speaker's attitude towards the subject under discussion. They range from discreet and precise tilts and bends, nods, dabs and flicks, to slashes, stampings and thumps on the table. Timed to lay stress on your most significant word or argument—and indicated by the size, speed and dynamics of these movements—they reveal exactly how you feel about the matter in hand.

Social gestures

As a social animal influenced by the conditions of communal living, human beings have developed a gestural language—almost, but not entirely, universal—that reflects the relations between people and their classes of society. The many forms of etiquette, those manners that are required or recognised within a society, have bequeathed us whole codes of social gestures. Even if we compared only the greetings and farewells current today among the different cultures and nationalities, with what we know about the gestures practised by people of earlier times through their art, history and literature, we are dealing with a very rich movement code indeed.

Again, these acts are so commonplace that it is easy not to realise how many finely-detailed adjustments we make to those gestures—that distinguish, for instance, between people we are meeting for the first time and those we know well; that make clear the formality or informality of the occasion; that indicate the status of the person we are meeting; that show the degree of intimacy that exists or that we would like to make happen; and that reveal or conceal the emotional significance of an event or the objectives we secretly entertain.

A handshake is so much more than the hand-to-hand action. The complete action includes some delicious body details. Who starts the gesture and at what speed do both of you take part? One hand or two? Feet together or apart? If one hand, what is the other hand doing? How many shakes and for how long is the hand-grip held? Who breaks the grip first? Does the shake involve the fingertips or the whole hand? How hearty, languid, yielding, reluctant, business-like or sensual is the message? What distance is chosen as the most appropriate for the circumstances? Do the bodies remain unengaged and upright, relaxed and active, direct or indirect? Do the bodies bow?

Bows and curtsies have developed an incredible range of expression between social groups over the centuries: everything from full prostration, one or both knees to the ground, elaborate turned-out leg positions complete with arm flourishes, to the merest drop of the eyelid and an inclination of the head; from the dairymaid bob and a demi-plié hidden under hoops and skirts to a full-curtsied reverence. All are subtly distinguished to comply with the social mores of the time and place.

Another intriguing thing is the thousands of ways you can make your props extensions of these gestures. You may no longer shake your spear or lay your club upon the ground or carry palms and branches to greet your visitors; ladies no longer rely on the language of fans, parasols and nosegays to send their messages across the room; nor do the men of today call on their handkerchiefs, hats and dress-swords to make an impression. Nor can the taking off of a single glove say as much as it once did. Instead, today's props, like cigarettes, beer-cans, joints, coffee cups, tea spoons, wine glasses, lipsticks, have become integral to our contemporary gestural patterns and can be as resonant.

Ritual gestures

Whatever else we have gained in this past century, we have also lost a range of observances that in previous centuries were important aspects of the lives of citizens of every class. In abandoning these social rites and ceremonies we have also dispensed with many of the ritualistic gestures that accompanied them. In doing so, we reflect the more egalitarian times we live in, but are also rejecting much of the metaphor and allegory previously present in the daily life and art of people from the past.

Ritual gestures are not literal, casual, domestic, impulsive or personalised. They are not prompted by random impulses. They are there to be performed, whether or not the participants know their origin or their meaning. There may be dynamic differences in the ways individuals perform them, but the form of each and its special energy and quality have become set over time, affirming the participant's conformity to all the ritual stands for. They are not expressive of the individual but connect them to the functions and duties they are swearing to undertake, and transform them into an embodiment of rank and responsibility, whether that be a prince becoming a king or a girl becoming a wife.

Some long-lived institutions, like royalty, the papacy, the judicial system, the armed forces and tribal life, still manage to maintain a lot of their ceremonial aspects. Celebratory events can also include various rituals. Weddings, birthday parties and anniversaries at which the wedding kiss and the exchange of vows and rings, the cutting of the cake, the proposing and drinking of toasts, the *Auld Lang Syne* chorus, are the high points of the occasion. Further examples include victory salutes and investitures, the Oscars, Emmys and Logies; trophies and prizes of every sort for events as varied as the primary school swimming carnival, the Olympics, the Grand Prix and State of Origin games; initiations, liturgies of worship and supplication; speech days and funerals and occasions of mourning.

Long before the praying and kneeling and signs of the cross had the least significance for me at the early communion service each Sunday morning in Wauchope's old and tiny weatherboard St Matthew's Anglican Church, the rituals, plus the singing, the dressing up—and I must add, the wonderful, unintelligible language of the psalms and the King James Bible—were sufficient to give me a sense of participation and make me feel bonded to something indefinable. The power contained in ritualistic gesture staggers me. The effect on the mind and emotions of the clasped hands and the bowed and kneeling body at prayer is rich enough in itself, but richer still when our own gesture is being shared by everyone in the congregation.

There's no need to search further for examples of the dreadful power that conformity to a sequence of ritual gestures can engender than by watching footage of the Hitler rallies or a political protest. Here, the unison rhythm and the uniform responses turn a group of individuals into a mob, with a mob's mind, a mob's energy and a mob's blind strength and dangerous certainty.

A rare opportunity to witness the actual consummation and birth of a ritual of demonstration and revolt came my way on my only visit to Tokyo. A group of us being shown over Tokyo University found our progress blocked by a rally of thousands of students protesting against a governmental decision.* Over the couple of hours we were trapped on the campus I watched as the protest-leaders worked the throng into rising anger, first by speeches and argument, then by drilling them

---

* This was one of a hundred student rallies during the 1960s protesting the US occupation of Okinawa, which was a staging post for troops to the Vietnam War, and domestic issues, including law covering medical practitioners. In January 1969 students occupying the university's Yasuda Hall were removed by the police using tear gas. Through the 1970s students actively supported farmers deprived of their land by the government decision to build Narita Airport, which was completed in 1978. A number of students and police were killed in these confrontations.

with the chanting of slogans and the waving of banners and effigies. Finally and most terrifyingly, they incited a hypnotic rhythm of unison gestures involving fists, punches and percussive actions, so aggressive and symbolic of violence that the spectacle became a trance-like, ecstatic dance of hate.

At each stage of the incitement, the individuals handed themselves over more and more fanatically to a mob state, and by the time the gestures were learned the students had reached a stage of hysterical solidarity that gave each a feeling of enlargement within the invincible power of the mob. Not until the leaders judged the individuals to have surrendered totally was the signal finally given to leave the campus. I would have believed any appalling story of death and destruction that might have occurred as a consequence of that march.

As a Movement director I have often needed to research ritual gestures authentic for the times and settings provided by the author, or to adapt and invent ones that could be accepted as authentic. Real ones can be less effective theatrically and can overpower or slow down other aspects of the production. If, for instance, in a production of a Jacobean or Restoration play, the director and his Movement adviser chose to stick to all the courtesies and protocol practised in those times, the dramatic action could be retarded and the procedures become tiresome to a modern audience. Invented ones need to be based on whatever evidence the text, its period and circumstances can offer but they work best when the creator succeeds in convincing the audience they have appropriate logic, satisfying theatricality and a style so consistent with the total concept that they would never dispute their authenticity.

In history, social gestures of respect and acknowledgment were at times formalised to a degree that made them virtually ritualistic. A famous example is the protocol of constant attendance that Louis XIV imposed on the French aristocracy at the court of Versailles. From the King's awakening in the morning till his retiring at night, he and his courtiers lived a life of rigid formality. The language of bows and curtsies; acknowledgments; greetings and farewells; the use of accessories like

fans, gloves, hats, swords, handkerchiefs, nosegays, cloaks, wigs and
headdresses; courtly behaviour and,
of course, the dances and the order
of their presentation served to fix
them in their levels of seniority and
favouritism, all ensured Louis' pre-
eminence and saw to it that order
was maintained and the King kept
them under surveillance.

I am aware that distinguishing
rituals from the routines of our daily
lives is a grey area. But arguing the
distinctions is less important than
noting the fact that they exist, and
including them in our exploration of
Movement. At yet another of those
eisteddfod events I once regularly
attended, we, in the audience, were

Tony Taylor and John Howard in *Nicholas
Nickleby*: Dir. Richard Wherrett, Movement
Keith Bain, Sydney Theatre Company 1983.

required by custom and good manners to applaud so many items
of performance, announcement, dignitaries, sponsors, prize-givers,
speeches of congratulation and thanks, that it became difficult to be
sure whether this accepted practice of clapping our two hands together
was a ritual, a convention or a social gesture. By the end of the night,
I had recognised a variety of responses within me, all more important
than the action itself. Some of my applause was as dutiful and formal
as any convention or ritual might be. Some of it was a genuine response
to the pleasure that my favourite parts of the program gave me. And
then again I clapped a lot of work that frankly bored me; and some
gestures were a shameless lie as I was seen applauding a decision
of the judges that shocked me. I wonder if it was evident to anyone
watching me how many of my real feelings could be read through the
hand-clapping I did that night.

John Howard and Tony Taylor in *Nicholas Nickleby.* Dir. Richard Wherrett, Movement Keith Bain, Sydney Theatre Company 1983.

Characteristic gestures

I give this name to the gestures that have become our personal motifs, so frequently and typically do we use them. These are the ones that make us feel most at ease and match our temperament and self-image. They often combine elements of our essence that unconsciously show through, while other elements cover qualities you would prefer the world not to see. They are especially interesting when we recognise them as being both our truth and a lie. While they contribute to what we might call our personal style, we tend to favour them to the point of over-use.

They take many forms. For some of us, it is an angle or position of the head, looking more out of one eye than another, perhaps angling the face upward or downwards, giving the effect of looking down the nose or up from under the brows. It can be something special you do with your face and features—how much or how little you smile or pull down the mouth. It is very much about the play of the hands and the use of the fingers. For instance, you may be characterised by your open-handed, spread-fingered, out-facing hand gestures while another holds their closed-fisted hands well against their body. You might keep your weight so far forward that you are virtually leaning toward your companions. Others maintain a space around them, sitting deep into the back of the chair or registering the world from a backward stance as they stand inclined over the back foot. Some are set at ease by holding a lapel, playing with their beads or twisting the rings on their fingers.

I include in this category body-gesture habits that derive from your chosen dynamic centre and whatever part gives you the strongest sense of identity. Nothing builds up your pattern of characteristic gestures as efficiently as your self-image, fed by those things you like and value about yourself, and those you hate or to which you give little value. Make these comparisons: the physicality, bearing, gestures and dynamics of a woman who loves being tall and considers her hair and her hips to be her best assets, compared with one who, has allowed childhood embarrassment about her height, the size of her feet, the length of her arms or her awkwardness, to overshadow her considerable artistic skill and intelligence. Compare her then with another woman who is accepting of her unspectacular figure, and comfortable with the colouring and the features that God gave her, and who is aware of the greater value of her competence, optimism and stable temperament.

I have a dear friend who survives on a diet of two recurring characteristic gestures. She constantly makes circles in the air with her hands, interrupting them only to tuck her hair unnecessarily behind her ears. The circles that her gestures draw may vary in speed and dynamic but are only from the wrist, are quite small, and are delicately drawn in the space just in front of her chest. At certain moments she will suspend the gesturing in a variety of asymmetrical hand positions to make a point of emphasis. Clearly, she has been using the gesture for years. It works comfortably, and well, for her in most circumstances. Yet she had no awareness of it till I mentioned it. The circling gives off a hint of fluency and elegance, the broken wrist line and the spaced fingers and open palms suggest a fastidious quality while the hair-behind-the-ear bit is quite emphatic and businesslike. Altogether the effect is charming. The combination of the two suits her and they are so distinctive and expressive of her nature that I would miss them if she decided to inhibit or replace them.

Mimetic gestures

We may not all be in the class of the great Barrault, Marceau and other masters of mime, but that doesn't stop any one of us from miming and mimicking our way through life. We suggest through gestures a range of actions, behaviour, characters, textures, moods and, of course, all kinds of non-present objects. There are two clear kinds of mime: one a theatrical technique of long lineage with distinct traditions of professional performance, the other a category of personal gesture we all employ in day-to-day living, either to accompany, and depict, what we have to say, or to communicate without the use of words.

The first of these groups boasts a proud history. The Movement-based arts of many ancient cultures include forms of mime as a dramatic means of retelling their myths and legends and giving them representational form. Mime remains a strong theatrical force in several modern societies and certain approaches to this wide subject are taught as part of the Movement program of drama schools everywhere including the Lecoq and the Decroux centres in France. The training they offer goes far beyond the time-honoured vocabulary of traditional illusive miming to finding personal processes of creativity; and this has led to distinctly new ways of producing physical theatre.

The second category of mimetic gestures is more spontaneous and is the one that fits best into this discussion. Since the miming will mostly be an accompaniment to a verbal account, the gestures set up rough, often sketchy drawings in the air. To this you may add personal touches, individual details arising from the unpremeditated nature of these gestures. This can have the dramatic advantage of revealing how you feel about the events and the people in the story. The mimed gestures accompanying a description of a prized and exquisite object will shape the hands and the whole body to express feelings of delight and appreciation as vividly as the spoken details of the object's shape, size and texture. Similarly, distaste or contempt is made obvious through expression, tensions and the dynamics of the body in action. Miming can also reveal hidden motives that are not innocent. It can be very good at exaggeration and excellent at ridicule.

Nervous gestures

In states of unease and heightened sensitivity or in conditions of mental and physical stress when 'nerves' are running high, your body will betray the resulting emotional state in a range of gestures that tell a story not intended to be told. You will seldom be successful at covering every trace of nerves that occur in the ordinary round of your life. The big test comes when something major with uncertain outcome crops up, like awaiting a doctor's report, an examination, an interview. Such situations produce a range of body gestures that are as familiar as chewing your nails or biting your lips; rocking, wriggling and squirming; fidgeting and using a variety of vibratory movements—blinking, tapping, fluttering, rubbing, wringing the hands, legs, shoulders and head; fiddling with objects, hunching and tensing the torso. Unsettling circumstances inhibit to some degree the sustained direct and free gestures typical of your calmer moments, forcing you to deal instead with the imprecise, bound and percussive movement that nervous energy engenders. Nerves make changes to your breathing patterns which in turn alter the shaping and tension of your body.

Few qualities are as enviable as the control I observe in those who survive such occasions with no trace of the nervous energy jumping around inside them. No giveaway facial or body expressions, no stumbles or stuttering, not one movement more or less than the performance demands, and no dint in the impression that the individual has enjoyed every moment of the situation. I take as a compliment any reference to apparent ease I have exhibited when I have succeeded in concealing under an outwardly relaxed manner the effects of a beating heart, a brain functioning like a flea circus, legs like jelly snakes and a belly full of bogong moths. It is easier to describe these nervous gestures than find the cure. However, there are enough therapies of centring, mind-body control, breathing techniques to provide help if you choose to seek it.

Stylised and rhetorical gestures

The theatre arts are a treasury of gestures that go well beyond the bounds of naturalism. And in a way all actors are exploring to some degree the processes of stylisation in all the roles they play. The range of this process extends from the slight adjustments that you make to your movement and speech so that they can be seen, heard and projected in the artificial conditions of a performance space, to a state of abstraction that is close to visionary. Rhetorical gestures make up a stylised language that is particular to the theatre, character or production. And like its vocal counterpart, the gestures are expressive, persuasive and extravagant. I have seen productions made memorable through the scale of the gestural detail and the extent of its elaboration, and I have been equally moved by others in which the stylisation was a matter of reducing movement almost to a stark stillness, to an averted or indirect focus, and patterns of movement that were more representative of geometry than reality.

Done for its own sake, without sensitivity to the rest of the production, stylised gesturing can be the most distracting element in a show. It can be movements fashioned to conform to a chosen or prescribed style of production, such as plays written in verse or elevated language. There are as many possible concepts for the presentation of any play as there are directors. Each concept, with its selected period and points of reference, might ask for departures from strict naturalism through techniques of distortion, enlargement, simplification or minimalism that would demand a form of movement appropriate to the concept. A light, fast, sophisticated comedy, a play for very young children, a melodrama, a piece of street theatre, a sci-fi action drama, a rock musical, a romantic operetta and a television soapie might deal with similar facts, feelings, people, moods and circumstances but the styles of gesturing that express these ingredients will differ, sometimes subtly, sometimes enormously.

One thing that is essential, and difficult to make happen, is a consistency of style throughout the full cast. Opera, in fact all musical theatre, calls on a gesturing style that accords with its extended musical and emotional phrasing, its metrical and dramatic rhythms, its heightened states of feeling, its conventions of repetition and elaboration. Added to all that is its dramatic structure of climaxes, musical interludes, solos, duets, trios, small ensembles or vast choruses, where all cast members need to be in view of the conductor, and placed so that the sound reaches its audience without interference. Compared to the body gestures of real life, the stage gestures of both principals and chorus in music theatre productions may seem to be artificial and lacking in truth. But stylisation at its best can lead to even richer expressiveness and take both the audience and ourselves even closer to the essence of the emotions being expressed.

I have mentioned that the truth of an inner life can often be better depicted by stylised departures from naturalism than faithfully observed gestures from life. Nevertheless, for the stylisation to have its effect, it needs to be rooted in natural truth, and the resulting gestures supported and justified by an appropriately vivid and focused inner life. Music itself is a good example of a stylised art, and movement that accompanies it calls for sympathetic treatment.

It is in the world of dance, therefore, that we see stylised gesture at its glorious best. The dance vocabularies of thousands of dance styles are composed of, and characterised by, body gestures that are stylisations of every form of natural movement. To these may be added further stylisations of movement already stylised and in their new form they are capable of carrying new meanings from their original source. They

Keith Bain as the Physician in Gertrud Bodenwieser's *The Imaginary Invalid*, 1950.

can be enjoyed aesthetically without concern for literal significance. They can be taught and learned without reference to their history. They can be improvised and invented, invested with some of the richest statements of which humans are capable, or performed for their own sake or for the indulgence of the creator and the performer.

In dance it is easy to see the techniques of the stylised gesture at work. To start with, it is only necessary to look at how the artistic manipulation of the elements of space, time and energy produce fresh effects of enrichment and abstraction. In terms of space, for instance, you can extend or reduce the distances and the range of the original movement material so that the gestures convey a more potent significance. New levels can be explored to carry stronger emphasis. What was static can be formed to make entirely new paths through the surrounding space in seemingly illogical ways that, instead, highlight the message and the meaning. Designs can be distorted, refined, exaggerated, minimalised. What was small can be enlarged.

Another process of stylisation is to rework the time values in gestural material by slowing or increasing the speeds of the original movement, lengthening or shortening the duration of the gesturing, breaking up the time of an extended phrase into the separate moments of which it is composed, transforming the dramatic rhythms of emotional gestures into metrical rhythmic patterns and vice versa.

Psychological gestures

Michael Chekhov's *To the Actor* is a revelation—some of it as clear as a bell, much of it complex and thought-provoking. Chekhov separated gesture as a basis for characterisation into two areas—physical gesture and psychological gesture.* The first is all the body gestures we employ on stage for the audience to read. The second is an overall body gesture the audience never sees. It remains your secret, the foundation on which your character is built. You develop it through improvisation as the archetype, the essence of the role, basing it on the qualities your intuition has led you to perceive. Through repetition of the body shape and all the details of hands, head, fingers, legs and feet which express the psychology of the character, you go deep into the inner life of the role.

---

*   First published 1953 by Harper & Row, New York. Latest edition London & New York: Routledge 2002.

I have my own version of this, to be used as an internalised preparation for those entrances that demand that you arrive on stage already filled with rich feelings, intentions and in full emotional flight. I often recommend that you find a characteristic gesture you would never allow the audience to see but which will generate the desired degree of emotion for the scene ahead:

- A series of strong taps on the breastbone to wake up the energies that will bring power, authority and pride to whatever follows;
- A couple of violent swipes through the air with clawed hands;
- A cringing body shape with hands hiding the face;
- A soft and sensuous stroking of the throat;
- A good punch in the guts;
- Kissing the back of your hand;
- Clutching or touching your genitals

—and hundreds more as bold and unsubtle as need be—anything to help place you in the appropriate state of mind for the scene about to take place.

I emphasise that these categories are simply one way of classifying the gestures we make in life and that actors must reproduce in their performances. Others may use different terminology and criteria. Call them what you like and classify them how you will but at least think about them, don't let them be accidental activities. The important thing is that classification helps you understand the differences between one gesture and another, and how to be more specific and discriminating in

One of the most exciting things is the nature and the reproduction of gesture. By gesture, of course, no one means waving your arms around. That is gesture but it is much more subtle than that. There's a turning of a head. To turn away from anything is a gesture. There are many different ways, at different speeds and pressures. And the thing that you turn away from is the thing that will spark movement, and the thing that they are turning to is the thing that may hold the movement. To understand the way in which the impulse of a gesture, and what it can mean in terms of performance, is only one part of it. Of course you must find out how to find that gesture in the moment, and if the gesture is stilted or contrived, or if it isn't arrived at in a spontaneous way, it creates a style. It's not automatically a bad thing but it creates a certain style.

RUPERT BURNS

your choice, leading you to deeper connections between the visible manifestation of the gesture itself and the impulses and inner sources that are the spark and cause. Ultimately what motivates the gesturing is a bigger issue for you as an actor than how a gesture is technically made.

8

Transformation:
The final touch

Keith's transformations were sublime. Those noble shoulders would collapse under the weight of indignity, that magisterial chest would contract into a cave of sorrow, the proud neck could no longer support that once bright visage, which now housed a collection of sad features, the dancing eyes now drooped like rain drops, and that wicked mouth had lost its wit. He showed us a little finger could be sad. A mouth can contain the fury of a thousand frustrations.

JEANETTE CRONIN

In some ways transformation is the magic moment when the artist succeeds in pushing back the narrow boundaries of the commonplace, the conventional and the purely personal and finds a newer, more intense reality of seeing and being. It asks you to surrender your everyday sensibilities and emerge into a freshly perceived reality where the values are richer and rarer, where images, ideas and symbols replace facts and figures, and aesthetic merit and abstraction are worth more than the natural and the literal.

The expression 'to transform' in theatre terms has several applications. As an actor you go through stages of transformation from yourself to the reality of another character by, for instance, learning first the lines given by the author and then the thoughts, intentions and motivations that lie behind them. A series of sentences does not bring a body to new life but a sequence of thoughts and a process of intentions certainly will.

In order to build your character the set, the props, the furniture and the costumes become part of your world. This process of transformation also extends to identifying your fellow actors as the characters they play, so that you can build your own character in relation to your world. For instance, in a scene between a father and son, if you first accept the other actor as your son you will play the father far more convincingly than if you concentrate all your efforts on your own transformation. If you can't convert your fellow actor into the son he must be, for your reality, you may never pierce the heart of the character. Surely, if you could believe in this transformation, with all the implications of the context and the story, it will be the closest step you could take to becoming that father.

The big step into this changed state is too big for some, its atmosphere too precious and rarefied for others. For those who never make it, it seems as though the act of surrender is too uncomfortable or too dangerous. For the fortunate, the facility is there to move quickly and un-selfconsciously away from yourself and into the hearts, minds and circumstances of imagined people. For others, the preparation for a metamorphosis is a long, intense process of introversive technique.

Even if your role is of someone who resembles yourself in almost every way, you and that character are not the same person. You come from different circumstances, want different things from life, and place different values on them. Your transformation may not depend on any adjustment of your own physicality, vocal mannerisms or behaviour. It must come from the strength of your imaginative belief in all that concerns the character in hand. And there have got to be points of difference, even slight and subtle ones, on which to concentrate as a basis for that belief.

All the technique in the world is insufficient entrance to the realm of transformation. I have seen, and trained, craftsmen and technicians of prodigious talent, whom I have found trapped inside their own persona, unable to go beyond the limits of self. Some actors get no closer to a transformed state than levels of impersonation, pretence, disguise and imitation. There is an element of all these in theatre performance, but these skills—and they certainly are skills—must not become the actor's limit. On the other hand, I have watched virtually untrained individuals in a state of such belief in their newly-imagined identity that they have lost themselves in the reality of their new world.

I first perceived that miracle of transformation when I watched someone as grounded and normal as my father offer his hand to my mother, and lead her onto the dance floor. He held her in a closed dance position and somehow, as if on a breath, their two bodies connected into one new unity as they moved into the figures of the dance in a way that was no longer walking, no longer ordinary. And when the music finished, when both the dancing and the transformation were over, they became just two people walking back to their seats, nothing more.

This transformation involves a surrender, a yielding. This stepping out of your ordinariness and into a new reality, the absorbing into your own body and persona of a fresh energy and intention that goes beyond your everyday experience, is thrilling. It convinces me that it is an essential aspect of every art form and every artistic endeavour, and is the evidence of real artistry. If only audiences could see what happens to that transformed creature who held them in thrall, as he or she steps off the stage and back into the wings.

I really think I was so lucky to have been around at that time when everything was changing. To be asked to do things without rules. The times made anything possible!
KEITH BAIN

INDEX

Page numbers in *italics* refer to photographs.

A short biography
of Keith Bain

MICHAEL CAMPBELL

Keith's childhood was spent in Wauchope, in country New South Wales, the eldest of three children. From an early age he knew he had an aptitude for social dance, but began professional life as a high school teacher. In 1944 he attended Armidale Teachers' College prior to a posting at Kogarah, an outer suburb of Sydney, where he devoured every aspect of the city's post-war cultural life. On subsequent country postings he enlivened church halls and community centres with his new-found enthusiasm for theatrical performance.

1954 saw him back in Sydney with a position at Liverpool Boys High and the opportunity to audition for a dancing role in *The Tempest* at the old Metropolitan Theatre, a community centre of the avant-garde. The role led to a meeting with the dancer Gertrud Bodenwieser, and with her encouragement Keith gave up teaching and, at the age of 27, began training as a professional dancer. Bodenweiser was one of the early pioneers of the modern dance movement in Europe and, before her arrival in Australia at the outbreak of World War II, was professor of choreography at the Vienna State Academy of Music and Dramatic Art where she worked with a diverse group of visual artists, writers and directors including Max Reinhardt and Oscar Kokoschka.

To subsidise his studies Keith worked as a dancer and choreographer in the early days of television variety shows, and taught at Arthur Murray's dance school. In 1960 he was Australian Ballroom Exhibition Champion, and in 1961 and 1962 Latin-American Champion. In 1984 the story of Keith's foray into the world of competitive dancing became the basis of a short work created by a group of National Institute of Dramatic Art students. The piece was taken to Bratislava, Czechoslovakia as part of the Intrapolitana Festival of Drama Schools and was the genesis for the young Baz Luhrmann's first film, *Strictly Ballroom* (now a stage musical).

Keith's contemporary dance career also blossomed, and he performed with Bodenwieser Ballet and Ballet Australia. After Bodenwieser's death in 1959, Keith, with Margaret Chapple, took over the Bodenwieser Studio in Pitt Street, and later City Road, Sydney. It became the centre of much of the city's dance activity and the preferred rehearsal venue for visiting international dance companies.

In 1959 Doris Fitton, a grande dame who directed the Independent Theatre in North Sydney, invited Keith to teach actors to 'move'. He just said 'Yes' and began the next week, but with no idea of how to go about it. This opportunity led him ultimately to NIDA in 1965 where he taught for over 35 years. There he developed Movement for Actors, a unique discipline central to an actor's training.

At the end of the 60s Keith found himself at the heart of Australia's cultural renaissance, which saw the emergence of a new national identity. Uniquely placed among a variety of arts, he worked with artists and directors across the many companies that blossomed in the new environment, including the Old Tote, Jane St Theatre, Nimrod and the Australian Opera. He also choreographed the landmark Australian productions *Jesus Christ Superstar* and *The Legend of King O'Malley*.

In 1968 Keith served on the interim dance committee of the Australian Council for the Arts in its first year and went on to chair the Dance Panel. Keith became the first president of the Society of Dance Arts in 1969, with the aim of unifying Sydney's disparate dance community, and providing a professional dance company for the city. The Dance Company (NSW), renamed the Sydney Dance Company in 1979, was the result. Keith was also instrumental in establishing the Australian Association for Dance Education (now Ausdance), and the annual Dancers' Picnic (now the Dance Awards).

Keith received many honours and awards including the Queen Elizabeth Silver Jubilee Medal for services to dance and theatre (1977), an Order of Australia Medal (1988) and an Australian Dance Award for Services to Dance Education (2003). He was inducted into the Australian Dance Awards Hall of Fame in 2011.

In person he was characterised by his generosity, incisiveness and a fascination with life and its revelation through the body. He was also known for the twinkle in his eye and his abundant good humour. Our great hope is that this book will act as his legacy to forthcoming generations of actors, so that they too may receive what has been his ultimate gift to all his students, permission to realise their potential not just as artists, but as people.

MICHAEL CAMPBELL

Since 1995 Michael Campbell has worked as an artistic director, CEO, artistic co-ordinator, events manager, librettist, writer, editor, director, choreographer and dancer, across the fields of literature, opera, dance and drama. Prior to this he was a principal dancer with West Australian Ballet, Queensland Ballet and Oper der Stadt Köln (Germany). In his role as director and choreographer Michael has worked for many Australian companies including Sydney Theatre Company, Melbourne Theatre Company, Bell Shakespeare Company and Griffin Theatre Company. Over the past twenty years Michael has worked for Opera Australia in various capacities including as director, revival director, choreographer, producer and set designer, working on productions as diverse as *Salome*, *La Forza del Destino*, *Merry Widow* and *Handa Opera on Sydney Harbour*. In 2004 he directed the opera *Madeline Lee*, which he also co-wrote; it was nominated for 7 Helpmann Awards including Best Opera and Best New Work.

Prior to taking up the position of Festival Director for the Brisbane Writers Festival (2006-2009), he ran Australia's largest bookshop-based literary events program at gleebooks in Sydney for 4 years (2002-2005). Currently he is working freelance as a director, choreographer, events manager, arts consultant, dancer, and as a freelance editor. Recent projects include directing the 40th anniversary production of *Equus* and the opera *Sir John in Love* by Ralph Vaughan Williams, developing drama scripts with young playwrights, presenting on the TV show *For the Love of Books* (Studio TV – Foxtel), judging for the 2012/13 and 2014 West Australian Premier's Book Awards, directing and writing *(she had) immortal longings* (both for the Australian Shakespeare Festival, Hobart), and editing *Keith Bain on Movement* (Currency House). In 2015 he will be directing *Cunning Little Vixen* for Pacific Opera.

www.ingramcontent.com/pod-product-compliance
Ingram Content Group UK Ltd.
Pitfield, Milton Keynes, MK11 3LW, UK
UKHW010047280225
455689UK00005B/77